D1035857

Marks

of

London Goldsmiths

and

Silversmiths

Georgian Period (c 1697-1837)

JOHN P. FALLON

ARCO PUBLISHING COMPANY, INC.
New York

5.95

Published by Arco Publishing Company, Inc.,
219 Park Avenue South, New York, N.Y.10003

ISBN 0-668-02663-4

Printed in Great Britain

CONTENTS

PREFACE

When, in 1363, it was enacted that every maker of silver should have a mark of his own to be stamped beside the 'King's Mark', the object was to prevent fraudulent practices which were rife at the time. The maker's mark on old silver is now of the greatest interest to the connoisseur and to the collector. Unfortunately, due to a fire in the Assay Office at Goldsmiths' Hall in the late seventeenth century the early records of makers' marks were destroyed, but from 1697 to the present day they are almost complete with only two books missing. Therefore the majority of London makers' marks entered during this period can be identified from the registers at Goldsmiths' Hall. What has previously been lacking, however, is a publication for easy reference which is both accurate and not too voluminous. This small book will supply the need.

The entries in the registers at Goldsmiths' Hall are in the form of inked impressions from the actual punches used by the makers and in most cases the signature and the address of the maker are included in addition to the date of entry. The illustrations which follow were traced from photographs of the original impressions and I can readily vouch for the care taken by the author to ensure their accuracy. To keep the book down to pocket size he has wisely omitted many lesser-known makers and instead included a bonus in the form of a number of biographical notes. Both the casual collector and the expert should find this book invaluable.

J.S. Forbes
Deputy Warden

Goldsmiths' Hall
London EC2
22.3.71

ACKNOWLEDGEMENTS

The author wishes to thank the following people for their assistance in compiling this book:

Mr J.S. Forbes, Deputy Warden) Worshipful Company
Mr J.C. Furmedge, Assay Office) of Goldsmiths,
Miss Hare, Librarian) London

Messrs Christie, Manson & Woods

Messrs Sotheby & Co

INTRODUCTION

For many years now, Sir Charles Jackson's book 'English Goldsmiths and their Marks' has been the standard work for identifying makers and their marks. In compiling his book he apparently did not consult the original records at the Goldsmiths' Hall since numerous discrepancies have occurred, presumably due to this lack of information. In recent years, as a result of increased interest and further research, some of these discrepancies have come to light, several concerning London makers and their marks.

Although it should be emphasised that the eminence of Jackson's work is not being questioned, the author hopes that this book, compiled from the original records at Goldsmiths' Hall, will help to rectify the inaccuracies, at least where some of the better-known London makers are concerned, and at the same time serve as a useful reference book giving some biographical details of the makers illustrated.

This book has been arranged in three main sections: a list of London Assay marks; an index of makers' marks; and a section on makers together with their marks and relevant information. To trace a maker by means of a mark, simply locate it in the index by looking up the first letter of the mark; this will give the name of the maker which can then be located alphabetically in the makers' section. Where more than one maker has the same name, numerical classification has been used for reference purposes. It must be remembered that, although this book contains over three hundred of the principal makers registered from 1697 to circa 1837, it represents only about one-third of those to be found in the records during this period.

Unless otherwise stated, all makers' marks illustrated in the book are accurate drawings of those entered in the records at the Goldsmiths' Hall, London. Those which have not been copied from the records were taken from actual articles of silver and the date given is generally that of the piece of silver on which the mark occurred.

All the drawings are from approximately one-and-a-half times to twice the size of the original punch marks. This means that where two or more different makers have used very similar marks to one another, for example the same initials in a rectangular surround, the only really conclusive check on the true maker is to compare the punch mark for size as well as shape with its original counterpart entered at Goldsmiths' Hall.

Makers and their Marks

Entries in the records were made by the actual metal punch used on the silverware. The punch tip was coated with a special ink and then pressed on to the appropriate page in the record book, thus leaving an ink impression of the punch mark. This was not always done very carefully with the result that some entries are smudged and blurred, while others are indistinct or have missed printing in part due to insufficient ink. It is because of this that drawings of the marks have been used as illustrations.

The earliest marks illustrated herein originate from 15 April 1697, the date when records were first kept in book form at Goldsmiths' Hall. Prior to this date, according to a work written in 1677 called 'The Touchstone for Gold and Silver Wares', lists of makers' marks were kept in the form of columns in the Assay Office at Goldsmiths' Hall. These marks were struck one below the other on to a column of hardened lead that was coupled with an adjoining column of parchment or vellum on which was written the corresponding maker's name. Records in this form are thought to have been in use for some two hundred years but unfortunately no example has survived to modern times. The columns were possibly destroyed when Goldsmiths' Hall was burnt out in the Great Fire of 1666 or probably in the Assay Office fire of November 1681. However, there still exists a copper plate with makers' marks stamped on it covering the period from 1675 to 1697.

8

Unfortunately, as this plate does not give the makers' names or dates of entry of their marks, one can only recognise those marks which are known from other sources or which have been re-entered as Old Standard marks in the written records after 1 June 1720.

On 25 March 1697, the standard of silver for wrought plate was raised from 92·5% to 95·84% pure; ie from 925 parts to 958·4 parts of pure silver in every 1000. This was known as the New Standard or Britannia Standard, indicated on silverware by a mark depicting the figure of Britannia. Under this new standard, which remained compulsory until 31 May 1720, the old maker's mark was prohibited and a new one required to be used composed of the first two letters of the surname. In many instances this mark has the letters 'N.S.' after its entry in the records, thus indicating that it was a New Standard mark.

When the Old Standard of 92·5% pure was restored on 1 June 1720, the old form of maker's mark, namely the initials of the Christian and surname, was resumed. This mark often has the letters 'O.S.' after its entry in the records, thus indicating that it was an Old Standard mark. At the same time, the New Standard with its corresponding marks was retained as an optional alternative for silversmiths to use whenever they desired. This continued until 1739 when New Standard makers' marks were abandoned, although New Standard silver remains in use to the present day. Thus, in many instances of silverware made between 1720 and 1739, it is possible to determine the standard of silver used according to the type of maker's mark stamped on the article.

In 1773, an inquiry was made by a Committee of the House of Commons as to 'the names and trades of the Wardens and Assayers of the Goldsmiths' Company, London, and when, at what time and by whom they were respectively elected.' The result of this inquiry was an account known as the Parliamentary Return of 1773, which contained the names and addresses of all Goldsmiths, Silversmiths, Plate workers, etc whose marks had been entered at the Assay Office and who were still active members of the Company on 8 March 1773. It also stated the trade of each person, whether it was Plate worker, Goldsmith and Gold worker, Spoon maker, Haft and Hilt maker or Candlestick maker. In order to draw up this account, volumes of the Goldsmiths' records were submitted to the Parliamentary Committee but apparently two volumes containing makers' marks were never returned. These consisted of Small Workers marks from 24 May 1739 to 13 July 1758 and of Large Workers marks from 30 September 1759 to 7 March 1773. It may well be that these volumes still exist today and are filed away with other records in the archives of Parliament, provided they survived the fire of 16 October 1834 when the old Houses of Parliament were largely destroyed. Because of the missing volumes, some silverware made during these two periods cannot always be attributed conclusively to a particular maker. However, one sometimes comes across a piece of silver made during one of these periods which is stamped with a maker's mark corresponding exactly with a mark entered at a later date. This is undoubtedly the same maker, his original mark being presumably in one of the missing volumes and for some reason, such as a change of address, he has entered his mark again at a later date.

Sometimes a maker's mark is found to be only similar to one entered in the records. In this case, provided it has a distinctive design already associated with that particular maker, one can usually assume it to be a variation of the mark already entered. Probably he did not bother to have it entered since it was so similar to the recorded mark and yet sufficiently distinctive not to be mistaken for any other maker. An example of this is to be found under the maker John Tuite. Occasionally a maker reverted to one of his earlier marks without re-recording it. Such a situation might occur after the termination of a partnership with another maker, which is what appears to have happened to Daniel Smith and Robert Sharp after Richard Carter disappeared from the partnership in 1780.

An article of silver stamped with a maker's mark could have been made either by that particular craftsman or by one of his journeymen in the workshop. Consequently, the larger the workshop, the more journeymen employed and the greater the likelihood that the Mastercraftsman only supervised the article's manufacture. Generally a maker, having already served an apprenticeship of at least seven years, had the ability to produce his own article of silverware, if so required. However, exceptions could and did occasionally occur. For example, a person who became a member of the Goldsmiths' Company by Patrimony had not necessarily served an apprenticeship, and the widow of a member who had recently died was usually permitted to take over her late husband's business without being a silversmith herself. In that instance, manufacturing would be carried out by the journeymen whilst she ran the design side perhaps or kept the books. Yet there are instances where women did serve apprenticeships and proved themselves competent silversmiths in their own rights. Where a widow has entered her own mark at Goldsmiths' Hall it is usually easily distinguished by its diamond-shaped surround, a design borrowed from ancient heraldry where widows' arms were enclosed in a similar frame called a lozenge.

Methods of Entry to the Goldsmiths' Company

Becoming a member or Freeman of the Goldsmiths' Company could be achieved in any one of three possible ways; by Service, by Redemption or by Patrimony.

1. **Service:** to serve and complete an apprenticeship to a Freeman of the Goldsmiths' Company. The period was generally seven years, sometimes more.

2. **Redemption:** to be nominated and seconded by members of the Goldsmiths' Company and then pay an entrance fee if elected by the Company's Court of Assistants.

3. **Patrimony:** to receive the freedom of the Company automatically upon application provided that the father, at the time of the child's birth, was already a Freeman. If the parent became free after the birth then the child could not claim freedom by Patrimony.

Occasionally a member of a Goldsmiths' Company in another part of the country wished to work in London and become a member of the London Company. Transference of membership was arranged through a Letter of Attorney giving proof to the new Company of existing freedom.

Structure of the Goldsmiths' Company

The general members of the Company were called Freemen. Above them was the Livery composed of approximately two hundred Liverymen who had been elected from the Freemen. One of their annual duties was to combine with the Liverymen of other Companies in the city for the purpose of electing the Lord Mayor of London. Over this group, governing the whole Goldsmiths' Company, was the Court of Assistants. In 1722, the Court consisted of sixty members but it was gradually reduced during the eighteenth century until in 1827 the number was fixed at twenty-five members. Within the Court, four Assistants were elected annually to serve as senior members called Wardens. These Wardens were also placed in order of seniority, namely fourth, third, second and Prime Warden. In structure, it was rather like a modern board of directors with the Prime Warden in the place of the Chairman. This board also appointed a Touch Warden or Deputy Warden who was in charge of the Assay Office and its workings. Before being elected to either the Livery or the Court of Assistants, a member asked to be nominated and then paid an entrance fee upon election. The same procedure is followed today, although the Court of Assistants has been substantially enlarged.

Originally any craftsman or tradesman working within London's city boundaries was required to be a member of a Company representative of one of the crafts or trades, eg Goldsmiths, Broderers, Turners, Watchmakers, Blacksmiths, Carpenters, etc. The fact that a craftsman was the member of a different Company to the one representing the craft in which he worked did not matter because, once he had gained the Freedom of any Company, and thereby the Freedom of the City, he was at liberty to work within the city boundaries at the craft or trade of his choice. Hence, several esteemed city Goldsmiths included in this book were not members of the Goldsmiths' Company but had gained their Freedom from other Companies. After the Great Fire of London in 1666, the Goldsmiths' Company, together with others, found it increasingly difficult to enforce this regulation with the result that the occasional maker who was not a Freeman did manage to work within the city precincts. Outside the city boundaries it was optional whether or not they became members and, for this reason, numerous makers with marks entered in the Goldsmiths' registers were not Freemen of the Company since they worked outside the city.

However, Goldsmiths were permitted to work within the city boundaries without being Freemen if they worked in certain districts of the city called 'Liberty Areas'. These were privileged regions within the City of London which, prior to 1697, were exempt from the jurisdiction of the city and its civil laws and possessed rights of sanctuary. Each area elected its own sheriff and gave freedom from arrest to persons within its precincts. These concessions were abused and the Liberty Areas became the resorts of criminals and miscreants, hence the privileges were abolished by Act of Parliament in 1697 and the areas were again brought under the jurisdiction of the City, although they continued to be used by craftsmen trading within the areas who were not members of a City Company. The Liberty Areas included St Martins-le-Grand (favoured by Goldsmiths because of its proximity to Goldsmiths' Hall); Blackfriars; Whitefriars; St Katherine's by the Tower; the Temple; Duke's Place, Aldegate and Tower liberties, Minories precinct.

Assaying

Then as now, all articles of silver were required to be sent to the Assay Office for testing to ensure that the correct standard of silver had been used. For this, scrapings were removed from the article, weighed, wrapped in lead foil, and then heated in a small cup called a cupel. This cupel,

13

being made of bone ashes, absorbed all the alloy metals leaving a residue of pure silver. The residue was weighed and the result compared with the weight of the original scrapings. If the difference was more than a certain amount, it meant that the silver was below standard and consequently the article was rejected. This method has now been superceded by a more accurate procedure for assaying silver.

In the Goldsmiths' Company, each assay year ran from the 19 May (St Dunstan's Day) to 18 May of the following year. This meant that every May a new date letter was introduced for the coming year which partially spanned two normal calendar years (eg May 1749 to May 1750). The procedure still applies today except that the change-over now occurs at a convenient time in mid-May.

Until 31 December 1751, the entries of makers' marks were generally dated according to a registration year which commenced on 1 April and finished on 25 March of the following year. At the end of 1751, the normal calendar year was introduced and is still in use today for the registration of marks. Thus prior to 1751, any mark registered between 1 January and 31 March was dated as having been entered in the previous calendar year, because the Office's new year started on the 1 April. It followed that the dates which actually occurred from January to March 1751 were given as 1750, but for the subsequent year these three months were given as per the actual calendar year, namely 1752. Because of this changeover, no registration dates were given from January to March 1751, as it was then 1752.

Apprenticeship and Freedom Records

In the following section, the dates of apprenticeships and freedoms were obtained from the actual records of the time, the majority of which are to be found at Goldsmiths' Hall. Most of these dates were taken from the Goldsmiths' records except where makers were apprenticed to or gained freedom of other city Companies. In those cases, the information has been obtained from records held by the pertinent Company or from the Guildhall library where

14

many Companies' records are now kept. Occasionally, the date when a maker undertook an apprenticeship can be traced without finding any record of his freedom date, usually about seven years later. This is generally due to the fact that he never completed his apprenticeship. Again, in rare instances, his freedom date is missing because he became free of another Company and this is often discovered solely by noticing his name in the records of that other Company. In the Guildhall library are preserved London Directories, records of censuses taken at irregular intervals during the eighteenth century, listing the names and addresses of all tradesmen in the city. It is sometimes possible to trace a Goldsmith or Silversmith in these Directories in order to discover if he was still trading at a particular time and occasionally there is a clue suggesting the Company of which he was a Freeman. While the apprenticeship and freedom records at Goldsmiths' Hall are comprehensive, those of some other Companies are depleted, books having been misplaced over the years, destroyed by general deterioration, local fires or bombing during the last war.

REFERENCES

English Goldsmiths and their Marks by Sir Charles J. Jackson
Old English Plate by Wilfred Joseph Cripps
The London Goldsmiths by Ambrose Heal
Hester Bateman by David S. Shure
Paul Lamerie by Philip A.S. Phillips
Paul Storr by N.M. Penzer
Barraud by E.M. Barraud
The Lengthening Shadow of Rundells by Shirley Bury
The Phipps Family & Edward Robinson by Sir Eric Sachs
Huguenot Goldsmiths in England & Ireland by Joan Evans
The Hennells Identified by Percy Hennell
   (Connoisseur Magazine, December 1955)
The Copper Plate of the Goldsmiths Company of
   Newcastle-upon-Tyne by J.W. Clark
Ancestors and descendants of Peze Pilleau the
   London Goldsmith by C.T. Clay
The Goldsmiths' Company, London for records of
   apprenticeships, freedoms, makers marks and Court
   minutes
The following companies for records of apprenticeships
   and freedoms:
   The Blacksmiths' Company
   The Brewers' Company
   The Broderers' Company
   The Butchers' Company
   The Clothworkers' Company
   The Girdlers' Company
   The Haberdashers' Company
   The Longbow String Makers' Company
   The Merchant Taylors' Company
   The Pewterers' Company
   The Skinners' Company
   The Wax Chandlers' Company

24 June 1763
Noble Street
Moved to Oat Lane
26 February 1765

5 October 1767
Oat Lane, Noble Street

10 May 1769
Oat Lane, Noble Street

15 October 1779
5 Oat Lane
Small worker

1 September 1784
5 Oat Lane, Noble Street
Plate worker

15 September 1790
5 Oat Lane, Noble Street
Plate worker

17

16 October 1790
5 Oat Lane, Noble Street

Removed to 11 Wilson Street, Finsbury
3 February 1821

William Abdy (No 1) obtained his freedom of the
Goldsmiths' Company by Redemption on 2 July 1752.

He was made a Liveryman in June 1763 and died at some
time before 1796.

His two sons William (No 2) and John obtained their
freedoms by Patrimony on 4 April 1781 and 4 October
1786 respectively.

William (No 2) was made a Liveryman in February 1791
and eventually resigned from the Company on 3 December
1823.

It seems that William (No 2), after obtaining his freedom,
worked with his father and eventually took over the firm.
This possibly occurred in 1784 when new marks were
entered in the records noting him as a plate worker
instead of a small worker. In this case all marks from 1784
onwards could be William (No 2).

11 May 1731
with George Hindmarsh
Christopher's Court,
St Martins-le-Grand

5 October 1731
Living in new Rents,
St Martins-le-Grand

23 June 1739
O.S.
In new Rents, St Martins-le-Grand

April 1740
N.S.
In new Rents, St Martins-le-Grand

He was not apprenticed through the Goldsmiths' Company
nor was he a Freeman of the Company.

His address of St Martins-le-Grand, although within the
city, was known as a "liberty" area which meant it was
exempt from the city's civil laws. Because of this he was
not obliged to be a Freeman of a Company while trading
in this locality.

(No date) (Probably February) 1759
with William Jury
Lilypot Lane

29 October 1759
with William Jury
Lilypot Lane

8 October 1760
Lilypot Lane

23 February 1762
Lilypot Lane

11 January 1764
St Anns Lane

4 April 1765
St Anns Lane

15 May 1766
St Anns Lane

18 June 1767
St Anns Lane

15 August 1769
St Anns Lane

5 February 1774
3 St Anns Lane
Buckle Maker

26 March 1776
3 St Anns Lane

30 May 1781
3 St Anns Lane

6 March 1782
3 St Anns Lane

24 February 1787
3 St Anns Lane

5 February 1802
3 St Anns Lane

He was a Freeman of the Loriners' Company but not of
the Goldsmiths' Company.

His son, Stephen (No 2) obtained his freedom of the
Goldsmiths' Company in 1784 and entered his own
marks concurrently with Stephen (No 1) from the same
address.

24 May 1792
3 St Anns Lane
Buckle maker

21 May 1795
3 St Anns Lane

17 June 1807
3 St Anns Lane

14 November 1813
3 St Anns Lane
Plate worker

2 May 1815
St Anns Lane

Removed to 8 Wingrove Place,
Clerkenwell, 13 March 1824

Removed to 70 Chapel Street, Islington,
21 January 1825

He was the son of Stephen Adams (No 1) and was
apprenticed to Joseph Walton on 1 October 1777. He
obtained his freedom on 6 October 1784, was made a
Liveryman in February 1791 and died on 15 July 1840.

Apparently he worked from the same premises as his
father since his first three marks were entered
concurrently with Stephen (No 1) and were from the
same address.

19 August 1775
with Henry Green
62 St Martins-le-Grand
Plate workers

20 September 1786
18 Aldersgate Street
Plate worker

25 September 1789
18 Aldersgate Street

He was the son of Charles Aldridge and was apprenticed
to Edward Aldridge (Clothworker) on 5 July 1758.
Possibly Edward was his uncle. He obtained his freedom
of the Goldsmiths' Company on 5 February 1766. His
partnership with Henry Green at Aldersgate Street was
listed in the Parliamentary Return of 1773 so presumably
an earlier mark to that of 1775 was entered in one of the
missing volumes of marks. Charles junior also had a
brother, Edward, who was apprenticed to Edward
(Clothworker) on 8 March 1750 and obtained his freedom
on 5 April 1758. This Edward junior was made a Liveryman in July 1763 and died between 1802 and 1811.

5 February 1723
St Leonard Court, Foster Lane

29 June 1739
Lillypot Lane
Clothworker
20 April 1743 removed to Foster Lane
Removed to Foster Lane
20 April 1743

20 July 1753
with John Stamper

He was never a Freeman of the Goldsmiths' Company. He
was the son of William Aldridge and obtained his freedom
of the Clothworkers' Company by Patrimony on 4
February 1723.

In June 1742 he and five other goldsmiths were charged
with counterfeiting assay marks on wrought plate to avoid
paying duty and assay charges. By August 1742, he had
been prosecuted, tried and acquitted of the charge against
him.

Two relatives who were apprenticed to him were Edward
and Charles Aldridge in 1750 and 1758 respectively.
Possibly they were his nephews.

Edward obtained his freedom in 1758 and Charles in 1766.

William Plummer was apprenticed to him in 1746.

24

9 November 1729
with Mordecai Fox

Living in St Swithin's Lane, near
Lombard Street

21 August 1739
with Mordecai Fox

At the Sun in St Swithin's Lane

He was never a Freeman of the Goldsmiths' Company.
Possibly he was a Freeman of another Company thereby
permitting him to trade within the city precincts.
His partner, Mordecai Fox, was apprenticed to silversmith
Francis Garthorne who was a member of the Girdlers'
Company. Fox therefore became a member of the same
Company when he obtained his freedom on 15 July 1712.

J·A

20 May 1761
Featherstone Street, Bunhill Row
Later moved to Old Bailey.

He was the son of John Allen and was apprenticed to
John Pierce on 6 March 1744—45.
He obtained his freedom on 7 December 1757.

7 October 1811
55 Compton Street, Clerkenwell
Plate worker

8 April 1824
55 Compton Street, Clerkenwell

31 January 1831
with John Angell

55 Compton Street, Clerkenwell
Plate workers

6 July 1840
with Joseph Angell (No 2)

55 Compton Street, Clerkenwell
Plate workers

Removed to 25 Panton Street,
Haymarket,
13 October 1842

He was a weaver who changed his trade to silversmithing
before 1808 and entered his own mark in 1811.
He had three sons, Joseph (No 2), John and Abraham.
Joseph (No 2) was apprenticed to Henry Nutting on 5
October 1796 and obtained his freedom on 3 October
1804. He was made a Liveryman in February 1825 and
died in 1850. He entered a joint mark with his father in 1840
after his brother John had left the partnership. John, who
had obtained his freedom in 1807, had originally entered
a joint mark with his father in 1831, but in 1840 he took
adjoining premises and entered a new mark in partnership
with his son, George. Abraham was apprenticed to his
brother Joseph (No 2) on 6 July 1808. There is no record
of his having obtained his freedom.

26 July 1771
with Ann Smith
Aldersgate Street

He was the son of George Appleton and was apprenticed
to James Waters on 2 August 1751. He obtained his
freedom on 7 March 1759.

9 March 1720—21 N.S.
At the Golden Cup, in
Green Street
Freeman of the Butchers' Company

2 November 1722 O.S.
Green Street
Later he removed to Hemings Row

27 June 1739
At the Golden Cup,
Coventry Street,
Piccadilly

He was never a Freeman of the Goldsmiths' Company.
He was the son of Peter Archambo and was apprenticed
to Jacob Margas, a member of the Butchers' Company, on
6 April 1710. He obtained his freedom of the Butchers'
Company on 7 December 1720 and died in 1767. His son
Peter (No 2), was apprenticed to him and Paul De Lamerie
in December 1738 and made free in February 1747—48.
Peter Meure was apprenticed to Peter (No 1) and obtained
his freedom of the Butchers' Company on 5 July 1739.

18 January 1749—50
with Peter Meure

At the Golden Cup,
Coventry Street

He was the son of Peter Archambo (No 1), a member of
the Butchers' Company, and was apprenticed to both his
father and Major Paul De Lamerie on 5 December 1738.
He obtained his freedom of the Goldsmiths' Company on
3rd February 1747—48 and died in 1768, the year
following his father's death.

His partner, Peter Meure, was apprenticed to Peter
Archambo (No 1) and obtained his freedom of the
Butchers' Company on 5 July 1739.

1 November 1700

In Lombard Street

20 June 1720 O.S.

In Lombard Street

He was the son of Thomas Bache (Yeoman) and was apprenticed to William Harrison (Goldsmith) on 28 February 1672. He obtained his freedom of the Goldsmiths' Company on 5 March 1679 and was made an Assistant in 1703. He became 4th Warden in 1718, 3rd Warden in 1722, 2nd Warden in 1723 and Prime Warden in 1726.

April 1697

Catherine Wheel Alley,
Whitechapel

He was the son of Thomas Bainbridge and was apprenticed
to Robert Peak on 19 October 1683. He obtained his
freedom on 22 October 1690 and died in 1707 when
his wife took over the business and entered her own mark.

Mary Bainbridge

Widow of William Bainbridge
21 April 1707
Oat Lane

She was the wife of William Bainbridge and upon his
death took over the business entering her own mark
in 1707.

B Thomas Bamford

5 January 1719 N.S.
Gutter Lane

27 June 1720 O.S.
Gutter Lane

18 July 1739
Foster Lane

He was the son of Thomas Bamford and was apprenticed
to Charles Adams (goldsmith) on 18 August 1703. He
obtained his freedom of the Goldsmiths' Company on
5 September 1711.

Samuel Wood was apprenticed to him in 1721.

14 October 1808
with Rebecca Emes
Amen Corner, Paternoster Row
Plate workers
(These two marks were entered by "Virtue
of a Power of Attorney" and signed by
William Emes and Edward Barnard)

20 February 1821
with Rebecca Emes

Amen Corner, Paternoster Row

28 October 1825
with Rebecca Emes

Amen Corner, Paternoster Row

25 February 1829
with Edward Junior, John
and William Barnard

Amen Corner

Plate workers

Removed to Angel Street,
St Martins-le-Grand, 18 June 1838

His father, Edward Barnard, a silver flatter of Aldersgate, London, was born on 2 March 1735, married Mary Gastineau of London on 4 April 1763 and died on 23 February 1808. Mary, who had nine children, was born on 17 May 1734 and died on 30 April 1800.

Edward was born on 30 November 1767 and apprenticed to Charles Wright on 5 December 1781. On 4 February 1784 he was turned over to Thomas Chawner and on 4 February 1789 he obtained his freedom of the Goldsmiths' Company, remaining with the Chawner firm as one of its employees in the workshop. In the years that followed, he saw Thomas Chawner's son, Henry, take over the firm, then John Emes become Henry's partner. Eventually Emes became head of the firm with Edward as leading journeyman. After John Emes died in 1808, his widow, Rebecca Emes, took Edward into the firm as a partner. Edward was made a Liveryman in June 1811 and died on 4 January 1855.

On 28 January 1791 Edward married Mary Boosey, a cousin of William Boosey who founded the well-known firm of music publishers. They had ten children, five boys and five girls. Three of the sons, Edward, John and William, were apprenticed to their father to learn the trade of silversmithing. Edward was apprenticed on 7 February 1810, obtained his freedom of the Goldsmiths' Company on 5 March 1817 and was made a Liveryman in January 1822. John was apprenticed on 1 January 1812 and obtained his freedom on 6 January 1819. On 14 March 1826 he married Margaret Faraday, sister of Michael Faraday, the scientist. William was apprenticed on 5 July 1815 and obtained his freedom on 5 February 1823. Another son, George, became a landscape painter and art master at Rugby School.

Of the daughters, Mary married William Ker Reid, silversmith, on 11 February 1812; Elizabeth married David Reid, silversmith and brother of William Ker, on 26 August 1815; Sarah married Michael Faraday, the scientist, on 12 June 1821.

9 February 1737–8
at the Sign of Golden Acorn,
Chandos Street

26 July 1745
Cock Court, St Martins-le-Grand

27 January 1755
with William Sampel
New Inn Passage,
Clare Market

3 September 1755
New Inn Passage,
Clare Market

6 May 1775
with Thomas Morley

8 Albion Buildings

Plate workers

3 March 1780
8 Albion Buildings
Small worker

George (No 1) was possibly the son of George Baskerville (Yeoman) of Winterbourne Bassett, Wiltshire. If this is correct, he was apprenticed to Joseph Sanders on 4 May 1732 for a term of seven years, yet there is no record of his having obtained his freedom.

This is the only George Baskerville in the Goldsmiths' freedom and apprenticeship records for that period. Assuming this was the same person, he must have terminated his apprenticeship in February 1738 after less than six years in order to establish himself with his own mark.

Most likely some of these marks are those of his son, George (No 2), but which are his it is impossible to say on present information without further research. It could be that the son's first mark was that of 6 May 1775 when he commenced in partnership with Thomas Morley.

⊕ 2 May 1791
with Peter Bateman

Bunhill Row

Plate workers

 ⊕ (Between 1 and 3) January 1800
with Peter & William Bateman

 Bunhill Row

Plate workers

Born Ann Olympe Dowling in 1749, she was of Huguenot descent. In May 1769 when 20 years old, she married Jonathan Bateman. They had seven children including a Jonathan and William, both of whom were apprenticed to their father.

When Hester, her mother-in-law retired, Ann's husband and his brother Peter took over the family business. They entered their first joint mark on 7 December 1790. In April 1791 Jonathan died of cancer leaving Ann to carry on his share of the firm. On 2 May 1791, Ann with Peter her brother-in-law entered their first joint mark. Also during 1791 the family business moved to 108 Bunhill Row, the premises at 107 being let to an Adam Travers. In January 1800 her son William joined the partnership. In 1805 Ann retired due to increasing ill health from dropsy and eventually died circa 1814.

⊕ Mark entered in two sizes.

16 April 1761
In Bunhill Row

 9 January 1771
Bunhill Row

 17 June 1774
107 Bunhill Row
Spoon maker

 3 December 1774
107 Bunhill Row
Plate worker

 5 June 1776
107 Bunhill Row

 21 February 1778
107 Bunhill Row

 25 November 1781
107 Bunhill Row

28 June 1787
Bunhill Row
Plate worker

 3 August 1787
Bunhill Row

The daughter of Thomas Needham, she was born in 1709 at
Clerkenwell. In 1730 she married John Bateman, jeweller
and chain maker of 107 Bunhill Row. They had six children;
John, Letticia, Ann, Peter, William and Jonathan. John
the eldest, obtained his freedom in 1751 but never entered
a mark. He worked for the family firm until his death in
1778. Letticia married Richard Clarke, jeweller and goldsmith in 1755 and had six children who actually survived
infancy. One daughter Sarah, married Crispin Fuller, goldsmith. (For information on Peter and Jonathan, see under
their own entries).

On 16 November 1760, Hester's husband died of
consumption. Hester carried on the family firm and
entered her first mark on 16 April 1761. She appears to
have been illiterate, as her only signature in the records is
the crude initials H.B. In 1790, Hester handed over the
firm to Peter and Jonathan and retired to live at Holborn
with widowed daughter Letticia. In September 1794,
Hester died aged 85 years.

7 December 1790

with Peter Bateman
Bunhill Row.
Plate workers

9 December 1790
with Peter Bateman
Bunhill Row

The youngest son of Hester and John Bateman he was born
in 1748. Although he completed his apprenticeship to
Richard Clarke, his brother-in-law, in April 1769, it was
not until 7 April 1784 that he obtained his freedom of
the Goldsmiths' Company by Redemption. In May 1769
he married Ann Olympe Dowling. They had seven children
including a Jonathan and William (No 1) both of whom
were apprenticed to their father to become goldsmiths.
After Hester's retirement, Jonathan and his brother Peter
took over the family business and entered their joint
marks on 7 December 1790. In April 1791, Jonathan
died of cancer and Ann his widow took over his share of
the business.

Jonathan junior was apprenticed to him on 7 July 1784
and following his death, was turned over to Ann on 1 June
1791, eventually obtaining his freedom on 5 October 1791.

William (No 1) was apprenticed to him on 7 January 1789,
was turned over to Ann on 6 July 1791 and obtained his
freedom on 6 February 1799.

Benjamin Smith (No 1) was apprenticed to Jonathan junior
in 1791 and obtained his freedom on 6 February 1799,
the same day as William. (No 1).

⊕ Mark entered in two sizes.

⊕ 7 December 1790
with Jonathan Bateman

Bunhill Row

Plate workers

  ⊕ 9 December 1790
with Jonathan Bateman

Bunhill Row

  ⊕ 2 May 1791
with Ann Bateman

Bunhill Row

Plate workers

  ⊕ (Between 1 and 3) January 1800
with Ann & William Bateman (No 1)

Bunhill Row

Plate workers

  ⊕ 8 November 1805
with William Bateman (No 1)

Bunhill Row

Plate workers

⊕ Mark entered in two sizes

41

The son of Hester and John Bateman, he was born in 1740. In 1755 he was apprenticed to Richard Clarke, his brother-in-law but although he served the apprenticeship, he never took up his freedom of the Goldsmiths' Company. He first married in 1763 and lived at 86 Bunhill Row. He married again in 1776, his first wife having died, but he never had any children by either marriage.

Following Hester's retirement from the firm, Peter and his brother Jonathan entered their first joint mark on 7 December 1790. After Jonathan's death in April 1791, Ann his widow entered into partnership with Peter, their first mark being recorded on 2 May 1791.

In January 1800, Ann and Jonathan's son William joined the partnership and in 1805, Ann retired leaving Peter and William to continue running the firm. In 1815, Peter retired and eventually died on 19 November 1825 aged 85 years.

⊕   Mark entered in two sizes.

⊕ (Between 1 and 3) January 1800
  with Peter & Ann Bateman

Bunhill Row

Plate workers

⊕ 8 November 1805
  with Peter Bateman

Bunhill Row

Plate workers

15 February 1815

108 Bunhill Row

Plate worker

⊕ Mark entered in two sizes

The son of Ann and Jonathan Bateman, he was born in 1774. On 7 January 1789 he was apprenticed to his father to be a goldsmith but following his father's death in April 1791, William was turned over to his mother on 6 July 1791 to continue his apprenticeship. On 6 February 1799, he obtained his freedom and in January 1800 he entered his first mark in partnership with his mother and uncle. Later that year he married Ann Wilson. They had seven children, six daughters and a son William (No 2). In 1802 William and his family moved into 107 Bunhill Row. In 1805, his mother retired from the family business due to her increasing ill health from dropsy. Following his uncle's retirement, William entered his own mark on 15 February 1815.

In 1816 he became a Liveryman and in 1828 an Assistant. He was now living at Stoke Newington, the premises at Bunhill Row being entirely workshops.

He became 4th Warden in 1833, 3rd Warden in 1834, 2nd Warden in 1835 and Prime Warden in 1836. He again became 4th Warden in 1847, 3rd Warden in 1848, 2nd Warden in 1849 but failed to become Prime Warden again as he died the following year when 76 years old.

9 February 1827

Bunhill Row

Plate worker

(These marks for 1827 and 1830 were entered at Goldsmiths Hall by William (No 2) altho ugh, at the time, his father was still in control of the firm.)

22 May 1830
Bunhill Row

31 December 1839
with Daniel Ball

Bunhill Row

Plate workers

The son of Ann and William Bateman (No 1), he was born soon after their marriage in 1800. On 1 February 1815 William (No 2) was apprenticed to his father to be a silversmith and obtained his freedom on 4 December 1822. He did not get on very well with his father, particularly after marrying Elizabeth Parratt, a serving girl.

In 1829, he was made a Liveryman. In 1839 he assumed control of the family firm and took Daniel Ball as his partner.

He died between 1874 and 1877.

21 March 1750
Wood Street

He was the son of Richard Bayley and was apprenticed to
James Smith on 6 June 1732. On 13 February 1737 he
was handed over to his father for the residue of his term
with the consent of James Smith's executors. He obtained
his freedom by Patrimony on 2 March 1740.

29 March 1708
N.S.

Foster Lane

16 July 1720 O.S.
Foster Lane

19 June 1739
Foster Lane

He was the son of Antony Bayley and was apprenticed to
Charles Overing and John Gibbons on 28 April 1699. He
obtained his freedom on 11 December 1706, was made a
Liveryman in 1712 and an Assistant in 1732. He became
4th Warden in 1748 and Prime Warden in 1751.

Among his apprentices were Richard Gurney, Thomas
Cooke and Henry Brind.

His son was John Bayley.

1 October 1733
At the Unicorn in Henrietta Street,
Covent Garden

22 June 1739

Henrietta Street, Covent Garden

He was apprenticed to Jonathan Newton on 13 June 1722
and turned over to John Le Sage on 23 July 1725. There
is no record of his obtaining his freedom but presumably
he did not bother to take it up since he was working
outside the city precincts.

10 February 1759
Monkwell Street
Removed to Featherstone Street
31 October 1759

22 March 1763
Featherstone Street
Removed to Silver Street
3 April 1764

8 March 1769
Bridgewater Square

4 August 1772
Bridgewater Square

He was the son of John Bell and was apprenticed to
William Burton on 3 February 1747. He obtained his
freedom on 9 April 1755, was made a Liveryman in
March 1758 and resigned in August 1778.

21 July 1740
Eagle Street,
near Lyon Square

He was the son of William Bellaseyse and was apprenticed
to James Wilkes on 5 February 1733. On 27 July 1738
he was turned over to Marmaduke Daintrey and obtained
his freedom on 2 July 1741.

16 March 1716—17
N.S.
In Monkwell Street.
Freeman of Merchant Taylors

3 July 1723
O.S.
In Holborn.
Freeman of Merchant Taylors

He never became a Freeman of the Goldsmiths' Company.

He was the son of Richard Bellassyse and was apprenticed on 5 October 1709 to Seth Lofthouse, a member of the Merchant Taylors' Company who traded as a Goldsmith.

On 7 November 1716, he obtained his freedom of the Merchant Taylors' Company.

He died prior to 1733 when his son Charles was apprenticed to James Wilkes.

April 1697

Foster Lane

Free Brewer

(No date or address entered.
Possibly entered 10 July 1702 when
another maker's entry was written in what
appears to be the same ink)

19 June 1724 O.S.
Foster Lane
Free Brewer

He never became a Freeman of the Goldsmiths' Company.

He was apprenticed to a member of the Brewers'
Company and obtained his freedom of that Company on
19 June 1690.

Matthew Cooper was apprenticed to him in 1692.

8 October 1725
Gutter Lane
Free Goldsmith

5 July 1727
O.S.
Foster Lane

He was the son of Edmund Boddington and was apprenticed
to John Boddington and Giles Edmonds on 7 May 1706.
(John Boddington was presumably a relation). He obtained
his freedom on 5 May 1714 and was made a Liveryman in
March 1736.

Thomas Heming was apprenticed to him on 7 February
1737—8 but was turned over to Peter Archambo (No 1)
on the same day.

John Boddington

April 1697
Foster Lane

He was the son of John Boddington and was apprenticed
to Jacob Harris on 2 November 1677. He obtained his
freedom on 18 July 1688 and was made a Liveryman in
April 1705.

He became Beadle of the Goldsmiths' Company in 1714
and died in January 1728.

Edmund Boddington was apprenticed to him in 1706.

Pierre Bouteiller

13 February 1726—7
St Martins, South Court

He was not apprenticed through the Goldsmiths' Company
nor was he a Freeman of the Company.

John Bridge

13 November 1823
76 Dean Street, Soho
Plate worker

25 November 1823
76 Dean Street, Soho

He was a partner in the firm of Rundell, Bridge and
Rundell, jewellers to George III and his son George,
Prince of Wales. Paul Storr ran the manufacturing side of
the firm from 1807 until 1819 using his own mark on all
the silverware. When Storr left, Philip Rundell the senior
partner entered his mark at the Goldsmiths' Hall. When
Rundell retired in 1823, John Bridge entered his mark at
the Goldsmiths' Hall but never became a Freeman.

6 May 1742
Foster Lane

He was the son of William Brind and brother of Walter
Brind. He was apprenticed to Richard Bayley on 5 March
1733 and obtained his freedom on 6 May 1742. In
September 1746 he was made a Liveryman.

7 February 1748–9
Foster Lane

31 August 1751

Foster Lane

11 October 1757
Foster Lane

26 February 1781
34 Foster Lane
Plate worker

He was the son of William Brind and brother of Henry
Brind. He was apprenticed to John Raynes on 7 October
1736 and turned over to Henry Brind on 2 July 1742.
He obtained his freedom on 8 November 1743, was made
a Liveryman in March 1758 and died between 1795 and
1801.

16 August 1802
3 Red Lion Street, Clerkenwell
Case maker

23 June 1803
3 Red Lion Street, Clerkenwell

7 October 1805
with Richard Sibley

14 Bartholomew Close

Plate workers

6 July 1812
14 Bartholomew Close
Plate worker

10 August 1812
14 Bartholomew Close

23 April 1813
14 Bartholomew Close

He was not apprenticed through the Goldsmiths' Company
nor was he a Freeman of the Company.

N.S.

13 May 1721

Green Street,
near Leicesterfield

O.S.   Freeman of the Skinners

He never became a Freeman of the Goldsmiths' Company.

Born in 1698, the son of Isaac and Elizabeth Buteux, he was apprenticed to William West a member of the Skinners' Company on 4 December 1711. He obtained his freedom of that Company on 4 August 1719.

When he died in 1731, his widow Elizabeth Buteux took over the family business and entered her own mark.

15 November 1731
Norris Street, St. James

She was the wife of Abraham Buteux and upon his death
in 1731 she took over the business and entered her own
mark. About 1734 she married Benjamin Godfrey,
another goldsmith.

21 August 1740

Foster Lane

Removed to Carey Lane,
13 April 1741

13 December 1742

(No address, presumably Carey Lane)

Removed to Gutter Lane,
31 May 1743

He was the son of Giles Cafe and brother of William Cafe
and was apprenticed to James Gould on 15 December
1730. He obtained his freedom on 5 March 1740 and was
made a Liveryman in September 1746.

His brother William was apprenticed to him in 1741.

Thomas Hannam was apprenticed to him in 1754 and
turned over to William Cafe in 1757 due to John's death.

16 August 1757

Gutter Lane

Circa
1758

This mark is not recorded at
Goldsmiths' Hall.
Presumed to be William Cafe
and not entered due to its
similarity with the previous
mark.

He was the son of Giles Cafe and brother of John Cafe to
whom he was apprenticed on 11 March 1741. He was
turned over to Simon Jouet on 19 March 1746 and
obtained his freedom on 5 October 1757. In March 1758
he was made a Liveryman and he died between 1802 and
1811.

Thomas Hannam was apprenticed to John Cafe in 1754
and turned over to William Cafe in 1757 following John's
death.

April 1697
Gutter Lane

He was the son of Edward Canner and was apprenticed to
Francis Archbold on 18 June 1680. He obtained his
freedom on 20 June 1688 and was made a Liveryman in
April 1705.

His son Christopher (No 2) obtained his freedom in 1716.

Richard Watts was apprenticed to Christopher (No 1) in
1698 and obtained his freedom in 1707.

Christopher Canner (No 2)

30 May 1716 N.S.
Maiden Lane

8 July 1720 O.S.
Foster Lane

He was the son of Christopher Canner (No 1) and
obtained his freedom by Patrimony on 18 May 1716.

21 September 1776
Bartholomew Close
Plate worker

                30 October 1776

Bartholomew Close

                Left the trade (retired) 20 January 1777

He was not apprenticed through the Goldsmiths' Company
nor was he a Freeman of the Company.

Presumably it was his son Richard Carter who entered his
mark from the same address upon John Carter's
retirement.

20 January 1777
with Robert Makepeace (No 1)

Bartholomew Close

Plate workers

9 December 1778
with Daniel Smith
and Robert Sharp

14 Westmoreland Buildings

Plate workers

He was not apprenticed through the Goldsmiths' Company nor was he a Freeman of the Company.

Presumably he was the son of John Carter and entered his mark with Robert Makepeace on the day of John Carter's retirement.

It is possible that Richard Carter retired or died early in 1780, this being the date when Smith and Sharp re-entered the old mark of December 1778 but with Carter's initials removed.

BC
22 June 1732
At the Three Horseshoes, Pedlars Lane,
Charing Cross

20 June 1739
At the Crown and Pearl,
Bartholomew Close

19 May 1748
At the Crown and Pearl,
Bartholomew Close

18 February 1757
At the Crown and Pearl,
Bartholomew Close

He was not apprenticed through the Goldsmiths' Company
nor was he a Freeman of the Company.

His son was Benjamin Cartwright (No 2) a member of the
Blacksmiths' Company.

22 April 1754
Smithfield

7 September 1756
At the "Kings Arms & Snuffers,"
in the Strand

2 January 1770
Pall Mall

He was never a Freeman of the Goldsmiths' Company.

He was the son of Benjamin Cartwright (No 1) and was apprenticed to James Cartwright, a member of the Blacksmiths' Company, on 6 February 1745—46. Presumably James was a relation, possibly an uncle or older brother.

Benjamin obtained his freedom of the Blacksmiths' Company on 1 March 1753—54.

23 March 1739—40
Hemings Row,
St Martins Lane

He was the son of Jean Chartier and was apprenticed to
his father on 25 October 1720. There is no record of his
obtaining his freedom. Presumably he did not bother as
he was working outside the city precincts.

April 1698
N.S.
Hemings Row,
St Martins Lane in the fields

10 July 1723 O.S.
Hemings Row
Free goldsmith

He and his wife Suzanne Garnier were Huguenot refugees
from Blois, France. He obtained his freedom by
Redemption (by order of Court of Aldermen) on 13 April
1698. His wife Suzanne was related to Daniel Garnier the
goldsmith. Possibly she was his sister. Suzanne had three
sons, Jean, Daniel and Isaac. Jean, born in December 1697
does not appear to have become a Freeman or been
apprenticed through the Goldsmiths' Company. Daniel was
apprenticed to Jean senior in 1720 and although he
appears to have eventually taken over the family business
he never took up his Freedom of the Goldsmiths' Company.
Isaac, the third son, obtained his freedom of the Goldsmiths' Company by Patrimony on 2 July 1746. Jean
senior possibly had a daughter, Henriette. She married his
apprentice Alexis Pezé Pilleau in 1724. Pilleau had been
apprenticed to him in 1710 and taken up his freedom in
1724.

11 November 1786

Amen Corner

Plate worker

 31 August 1787

Amen Corner

 27 August 1796
with John Emes

Amen Corner

 Plate workers

He was the son of Thomas Chawner (Goldsmith) and
obtained his freedom by Patrimony on 7 December 1785.
He was made a Liveryman in 1791, an Assistant in 1801
and died in 1851.

14 April 1834

16 Hosier Lane
Spoon Maker

 25 March 1835

16 Hosier Lane

3 August 1840
with George William Adams

16 Hosier Lane, Smithfield

Spoon makers

She was the wife of William Chawner (No 2) and took over
the family business when her husband died on 20 March
1834.

Their son, William, who had been apprenticed to his father
in 1831, was turned over to Mary at this time and
obtained his freedom in 1838.

Circa
1763–4

These marks are not
recorded at the
Goldsmiths' Hall.

Circa
1765–6

They are assumed to be
Thomas and William
Chawner and were probably
entered in the missing
volume of Large Workers
marks.

Circa
1768–9

15 October 1773
60 Paternoster Row

1 November 1775
60 Paternoster Row

31 May 1783
9 Ave Maria Lane
Plate worker

C Thomas Chawner

He was the son of John Chawner and was apprenticed to
Ebenezer Coker on 4 December 1754. He obtained his
freedom on 13 January 1762, was made a Liveryman in
December 1771, and died between 1802 and 1811.

His son was Henry Chawner.

Among his apprentices were William Fearn, Thomas
Northcote, Edward Barnard, Henry Nutting and William
Sumner (No 1).

Thomas Chawner's partnership with William Chawner (No
1) at 60 Paternoster Row commenced circa 1763-4 and
lasted until 1773.

William Chawner (No 1) was possibly Thomas's brother.

William Chawner (No 1)

Circa
1763—4

Circa
1765—6

Circa
1768—9

These marks are not
recorded at the Goldsmiths'
Hall. They are assumed
to be Thomas and William
Chawner and were probably
entered in the missing
volume of Large Workers
marks from 1759 to 1773

17 November 1774
with George Hemming
Bond Street
Plate workers

15 February 1781
withGeorge Hemming

Old Bond Street

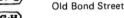

He never became a Freeman of the Goldsmiths' Company.
He was apprenticed to Francis Pigott, a member of the
Pewterers' Company and obtained his freedom of that
Company on 20 October 1757.
He was made a Liveryman of the Pewterers' Company
on 29 June 1761 but paid the necessary fine to be
excused as Steward of the Company in 1768 and again
as Renter Warden in 1777.
His partnership with Thomas Chawner at 60 Paternoster
Row commenced circa 1763-4 and lasted until 1773.
Possibly Thomas Chawner was his brother. In 1774
William went into partnership with George Hemming.
This lasted until circa 1790-1 when William probably
retired or died.

18 April 1808
with William Eley (No 1) and William Fearn
1 Lovells Court, Paternoster Row
Spoon makers

9 February 1815
16 Hosier Lane, West Smithfield
Spoon maker

13 August 1819
16 Hosier Lane

27 January 1820
16 Hosier Lane

14 February 1820
16 Hosier Lane

11 August 1820
16 Hosier Lane

11 June 1823
16 Hosier Lane

14 October 1833
16 Hosier Lane

He was the son of Jonathan Chawner and was apprenticed
to William Fearn on 4 January 1797. He obtained his freedom on 4 April 1804, was made a Liveryman in January
1824 and died on 20 March 1834. His wife, Mary, took
over the family business upon his death.

His son, William (No 3), was apprenticed to him on 6 April
1831. When William (No 2) died in 1834, his son was
turned over to Mary and eventually obtained his freedom
on 2 May 1838.

Pierre Le Cheaube

---

21 November 1707

In Pall Mall

27 June 1726
Living in Glass House,
Glass House Street

Free Goldsmith

He took out papers of denization on 20 March 1699.

He was the son of Thomas Le Cheaube of Metz, France
and was apprenticed to David Willaume (No 1) on 11
July 1700. He obtained his freedom on 21 November
1707.

20 April 1775
Fleet Market
Small worker

As the widow of Charles Chesterman (No 1) she carried on the family business following her husband's death in 1775.

Their son, Charles (No 2), appears to have taken over the business in 1780 when he entered his own mark following Ann's death.

Samuel Wheatly was apprenticed to Ann in 1777 and turned over to Charles (No 2) in April 1780 by consent of Sarah Chesterman the executor of Ann's will.

7 July 1741
Horton Street, Clare Market

 2 October 1752
Removed into Carey Lane

 20 November 1771
Fleet Market

He was the son of Thomas Chesterman and was apprenticed to George Greenhill Jones on 21 May 1734.

He eventually obtained his freedom of the Goldsmiths' Company on 2 November 1748.

In 1775 he died leaving his widow Ann to carry on the business. Their son was Charles Chesterman (No 2).

14 February 1780
62 Fleet Market
Small worker

6 March 1801
62 Fleet Market

He was the son of Ann and Charles Chesterman (No 1).

He was apprenticed to his father on 2 July 1766 and obtained his freedom of the Goldsmiths' Company on 4 May 1774.

His father died in 1775 and his mother in 1780.

25 September 1713 N.S.
Wood Street
Later of Lombard Street

23 June 1720 O.S.
Love Lane

15 December 1721 O.S.
In Lombard Street

He was the son of Francis Clare and was apprenticed to Nathaniel Lock on 17 February 1701. He obtained his freedom on 4 November 1712 and was made a Liveryman in October 1721.

His son was Joseph Clare (No 2).

2 March 1763
Deans Court, St Martins-le-Grand

16 September 1765

Deans Court, St Martins-le-Grand

1 October 1767
Deans Court, St Martins-le-Grand

He was the son of Joseph Clare (No 1) and was apprenticed to Jeremiah Marlow junior on 6 June 1732.

There is no record of his obtaining his freedom but this was not necessary as he was working in a "liberty" area. This was a locality which was exempt from the city's civil laws although it was within the city precincts.

31 May 1787

58 Featherstone Street,
Bunhill Row

Case maker

Removed to 126 Bunhill Row,
26 February 1789

Removed to 67 Wheler Street,
Spitalfield, 12 April 1790

27 January 1792
67 Wheler Street, Spitalfield
Case maker

18 April 1796
15 Ratcliff Row, City Road
Watch case maker

Removed to 4 Ship Court,
Old Bailey, 3 February 1800

27 November 1805
(No address. Probably 4 Ship Court)

He was not apprenticed through the Goldsmiths' Company
nor was he a Freeman of the Company.

Nicholas Clausen

10 June 1709
In Orange Street,
near Leicester Fields
Free Haberdasher

29 July 1720
O.S.
(Address as before)

He was not apprenticed through the Goldsmiths' Company nor was he a Freeman of the Company.

He obtained his freedom of the Haberdashers' Company by Redemption on 1 July 1709.

27 March 1738
Clerkenwell Green

25 June 1739
Clerkenwell Green

24 May 1745
Clerkenwell Green

20 December 1751
Clerkenwell Green

He was the son of William Coker and was apprenticed to
Joseph Smith on 21 October 1728. He eventually obtained
his freedom on 7 February 1739 when he had already
entered his first mark.

He appears to have been in partnership with a Thomas
Hammond but this was terminated in 1760.

In the Parliamentary Return of 1773 he was listed as a
Goldsmith of Clerkenwell Close.

April 1697
Foster Lane

He was the son of Hugh Coles and was apprenticed to
John Smith on 17 August 1660. He obtained his
freedom on 23 October 1667 and was made an Assistant
in 1698. He became 4th Warden in 1712, 3rd Warden in
1715 and 2nd Warden in 1716. Possibly he died in 1717
as he did not become Prime Warden that year.

7 June 1727
became Free Goldsmith
Foster Lane

19 October 1727
with Richard Gurney
At the Golden Cup,
Foster Lane

23 December 1734
with Richard Gurney
At the Golden Cup,
Foster Lane

28 June 1739
with Richard Gurney
Foster Lane

17 February 1748
with Richard Gurney
Foster Lane

30 July 1750
with Richard Gurney
Foster Lane

He was the son of John Cooke and was apprenticed to Richard Bayley on 11 June 1719. He obtained his freedom on 22 September 1726, was made a Liveryman in 1739 and an Assistant in 1752. He appears to have died about 1761.

Matthew Cooper

2 May 1702 N.S.
Foster Lane

13 July 1720 O.S.
Foster Lane

30 June 1725
O.S.
In the Minories

9 September 1725 N.S.
In the Minories

He was the son of William Cooper and was apprenticed to Robert Cooper his brother on 20 January 1692. At a later date he was turned over to Joseph Bird.

He obtained his freedom on 21 April 1702 and was made a Liveryman in October 1708.

April 1697

In the Strand

He was the son of William Cooper and was apprenticed to Thomas George on 8 January 1663. He obtained his freedom on 15 February 1670, was made a Liveryman in June 1682 and an Assistant in 1693. He became 4th Warden in 1707, 3rd Warden in 1711, 2nd Warden in 1712 and Prime Warden in 1717.

William Fawdery was apprenticed to him in 1686.

Matthew Cooper, his brother, was apprenticed to him in 1692.

John White was apprenticed to him in 1711.

At the Acorn in Drury Lane

(No date of entry given.
Presumably entered between
20 July 1722 and 8 December
1724, these being the
preceding and following entry
dates of other makers' marks
in the records).

He was not apprenticed through the Goldsmiths' Company
nor was he a Freeman of the Company.

Edward Cornock

14 July 1707
Carey Lane

25 November 1723 O.S.
Carey Lane

He was the son of Thomas Cornock (Taylor) and was
apprenticed to Henry Grant (Goldsmith) on 9 February
1697.
He obtained his freedom of the Company on 27 March
1707.

23 December 1708
Church Court,
St Martin's Lane

7 October 1729

Chandos Street

6 July 1739

Chandos Street
St Martins in the Fields

Goldsmith

The son of Julie and Augustin Courtauld, he was born
circa 1685 in France. He was one of four children of
whom only he and a sister survived childhood. His father
was born in France in 1661 and married his mother Julie
Giraud in 1677 when she was 16 years old. She died
between 1685 and 1687. His father then came to England
circa 1688 where he married his second wife, Ester Poitier
or Potier in 1689. They had one son, Peter, born in 1690.
This half brother to Augustin (No 1) also became a goldsmith. Augustin (No 1) probably came from France to
join his father in London in 1696 since he was made
a denizen on 20 July 1696.

He was apprenticed to Simon Pantin on 9 August 1701, obtained his freedom on 20 October 1708 and entered his first mark on 23 December 1708.

During 1708, he was contracted to marry Anne Ribouleau, presumably a relation of Isaac Ribouleau the goldsmith, but the marriage never took place. Isaac was apprenticed to Augustin (No 1) from 1716 to 1724.

About 1709, he married Anne Bardin and they had eight children of whom five survived their parents. One of the children, Anne, married a goldsmith John Jacobs in 1738. They had several children one of whom, Judith, married George Cowles, the goldsmith.

Another of Anne and Augustin's children was Samuel (No 1) who also became a goldsmith and had George Cowles under him as an apprentice.

In March 1751 Augustin's wife Anne died and the following month Augustin died.

Edward Feline was apprenticed to him in 1709.

1765   Not recorded at Goldsmiths' Hall. Presumed to be Louisa Courtauld and entered in missing volume.

   1768   Not recorded at Goldsmiths' Hall. Presumed to be with George Cowles. This partnership at 21 Cornhill noted in Parliamentary Return of 1773.

16 October 1777
with Samuel Courtauld (No 2)

Cornhill

Plate workers

Born at Poitou, France in 1729, she was one of a family of nine children.

Soon after 1730, she came to England and on 28 August 1749 she married Samuel Courtauld (No 1).

They had eight children of whom four survived their parents. One of them was Samuel (No 2) who was born on 20 October 1752.

In February 1765 her husband died, leaving her to carry on the family business. She is presumed to have entered her own mark at this time in one of the missing volumes of records.

On 8 May 1765, her husband's apprentice, George Cowles obtained his freedom, she having taken over his apprenticeship when her husband died. In 1768 George Cowles married her niece-in-law, Judith Jacobs, the daughter of goldsmith, John Jacobs.

In 1769, Louisa took George Cowles into the partnership and they entered their joint mark which is presumed to be in one of the volumes of records missing from the Goldsmiths' Hall.

On 16 October 1777, Louisa and her son Samuel (No 2) entered their joint mark, George Cowles having left the firm. Samuel, however, did not take up his freedom which was by Patrimony, until 4 March 1778. In 1780, Samuel emigrated to America so Louisa, then 51 years old, sold the business to John Henderson.

Meanwhile Samuel (No 2) married Sarah Norris Wharton, a widow in Philadelphia and eventually died near Wilmington in the State of Delaware in 1821. His wife died in 1836.

15 June 1721 N.S.
Litchfield Street,
St Anns, Westminster

21 July 1721 O.S.
Litchfield Street,
St Anns, Soho.

The only son of Ester and Augustin Courtauld, he was
born on 10 January 1690. His mother was Augustin's
second wife, the first having died in France, before
Augustin came to England circa 1688. One of the four
children by this first marriage was Peter's half brother
Augustin (No 1). Both he and his half brother were
made denizens on 20 July 1696.

On 20 March 1705, Peter was apprenticed to Simon
Pantin as was Augustin (No 1) before him. In 1709,
when 19 years old, Peter married Judith Pantin the
daughter of Esau Pantin, a goldsmith of St James.
Doubtless he was related to Simon Pantin.

On 3 December 1712 he obtained his freedom but did
not register his first mark until 15 June 1721. In 1729
he died when only 39 years old.

6 October 1746
Chandos Street
near St Martin's Lane

23 November 1751
Removed to Cornhill

The son of Anne and Augustin Courtauld (No 1), he was born on 10 September 1720. His sister Anne, married goldsmith John Jacobs in 1738 and had several children, one of whom, Judith born in 1741, married goldsmith George Cowles in 1768.

On 12 November 1734, Samuel was apprenticed to his father. On 6 October 1746 he entered his first mark at the Goldsmiths' Hall but he did not bother to obtain his freedom until 3 February 1747.

On 28 August 1749, he married Louisa Perina Ogier who was born at Poitou, France in 1729. They had eight children, one of whom was Samuel (No 2).

On 6 September 1751, George Cowles was apprenticed to Samuel (No 1).

In June 1763, Samuel was made a Liveryman and in February 1765 he died leaving his wife Louisa to carry on the family business.

10 July 1752
Foster Lane

 17 December 1755
Little Britain

 12 July 1758
Little Britain

He was the son of Edward Cox and was apprenticed to
Humphrey Payne on 16 January 1744. He was
turned over to John Payne on 13 March 1750 and
obtained his freedom on 2 July 1752.

In the Parliamentary Return of 1773 he was recorded as
a Goldsmith of Little Britain.

William and Albin Cox, his brothers, were apprenticed to
him in 1753 and 1763 respectively but only William
obtained his freedom in 1760.

C Joseph Craddock 'alias Cradock'

15 August 1806
with Thomas and Joseph Guest
67 Red Lion Street, Holborn,
Plate workers

24 February 1808
with Thomas and Joseph Guest
67 Red Lion Street, Holborn

Removed to 67 Leather Lane,
Holborn, 15 June 1808

8 June 1812
with William K. Reid

67 Leather Lane

Plate workers

19 August 1819
with William K. Reid

3 Carey Street,
Lincoln Inn Fields

24 September 1824
with William K. Reid

3 Carey Street,
Lincoln Inn Fields

13 October 1825
3 Carey Street, Lincoln Inn Fields
Plate worker

10 November 1827
3 Carey Street, Lincoln Inn Fields

He was not apprenticed through the Goldsmiths' Company
nor was he a Freeman of the Company.

Sebastian & James Crespel   C

Circa
1767

This mark is not recorded at
Goldsmiths' Hall.
It is thought to be
Sebastian & James Crespel
and was probably entered
in the missing volume of
Large Workers marks.

Neither Sebastian nor James Crespel ever became Freemen
of the Goldsmiths' Company.

Probably they were brothers who, from about 1762 to
1773, traded from premises in Whitcomb Street,
Leicester Fields.

By about 1778 they were mostly undertaking work for
the firm of Wakelin and Taylor (goldsmiths) of Panton
Street, Haymarket. In 1779 James Crespel's address was
given as Panton Street, Haymarket in the records at
Goldsmiths' Hall. This was on the occasion of his son
Honorius or Honore being apprenticed to John Wakelin
of Wakelin and Taylor. Presumably by this time both
James and Sebastian were working entirely for the
Wakelin firm. Sebastian probably retired or died at the
beginning of 1788 leaving James to continue on his own.

James had four sons who were apprenticed into the
silversmith's trade. Honorius and Andrew were
apprenticed to John Wakelin in 1779 and 1785
respectively. They obtained their freedoms in
1786 and 1792. Sebastian was apprenticed to
Honorius Crespel in 1801, turned over to Robert
Garrard in 1806 and made free in 1809 while James
was apprenticed to Thomas Gardner in 1803 and
made free in 1810.

(No date, (Between July 1720 and
December 1721) N.S.
Compton Street

(No date) Between July 1720 and
December 1721) O.S.
Compton Street
Freeman of the Longbow String

4 July 1739
At the Golden Ball, Compton Street,
St Ann, Soho

7 November 1740 N.S.
At the Golden Ball, Compton Street,
St Ann, Soho

22 January 1757
At the Golden Ball, Compton Street,
St Ann, Soho

He never became a Freeman of the Goldsmiths' Company.

Born in 1694, he was the son of Daniel Crespin of St Giles, Westminster.

On 24 June 1713, he was apprenticed for seven years to Jean Pons, a member of the Longbow String Makers' Company.

On 26 April 1721, he obtained his freedom of that Company by Redemption. This was by virtue of an order given by the Court of Aldermen of the City of London dated 25 April 1721. (See Longbow String Makers' Freedom records now held by the Fletchers' Company).

He and his wife, Mary Branboeuf, had five children: Magdelaine Benine born 1729 and later wife of Francis Barraud (watchmaker), Lewis Vincent Paul born 1732, Elias David born 1734 and later a clergyman in Guernsey, Paul born 1739 and Sarah born 1743. Both Lewis and Paul appear to have died young.

Paul senior appears to have retired in 1759 when 65 years old. He eventually died at Southampton on 25 January 1770 aged 76 years. His wife, Mary, died five years later on 15 December 1775.

31 August 1743
At the Crown and Golden Ball,
Compton Street

16 July 1746
Removed to the Golden Ball,
St James Street

16 November 1751

He was the son of Edward Cripps and was apprenticed to
David Willaume (No 2) on 8 January 1730—1. He
obtained his freedom on 2 May 1738 and was made a
Liveryman in January 1750.

Presumably he had died or retired by 25 April 1767,
when Mark Cripps his son entered his own mark from
the same address.

1 May 1775
with William Sumner (No 1)
1 Clerkenwell Close
Plate workers

27 January 1776
with William Sumner (No 1)
1 Clerkenwell Close

1 May 1777
with William Sumner (No 1)
1 Clerkenwell Close

27 January 1780
with William Sumner (No 1)
1 Clerkenwell Close

5 April 1782
21 Foster Lane
Plate worker

(and again)

12 November 1783
14 Giltspur Street

9 December 1785
14 Giltspur Street

6 January 1795
14 Giltspur Street

5 February 1802
14 Giltspur Street

4 May 1804
14 Giltspur Street

7 April 1807
with George Smith (No 4)
Giltspur Street

Spoon makers

2 January 1812
14 Giltspur Street

Plate worker

He obtained his freedom by Redemption on 1 May 1782.
Presumably this was necessary when he moved to within
the city precincts at his new address in Foster Lane.
He was made a Liveryman in February 1791 and died
in April 1815.

Circa 1767

These two marks are not recorded at Goldsmiths' Hall. They are assumed to be

Circa 1773

J. Crouch and T. Hannam and possibly entered in the missing volumes

13 April 1799
with Thomas Hannam
37 Monkwell Street
Plate workers

He was the son of Christopher Crouch and was apprenticed to Richard Rugg on 8 November 1758. He obtained his freedom on 4 December 1765. His partnership with Thomas Hannam was recorded in the Parliamentary Return of 1773 as being at 28 Giltspur Street.

William Frisbee was apprenticed to him in 1774.

His son John Crouch (No 2), was apprenticed to him in 1790.

11 February 1808
37 Monkwell Street
Plate worker

He was the son of John Crouch (No 1) and was apprenticed
to him on 6 January 1790. He obtained his freedom on
1 February 1797, was made a Liveryman in March 1829
and died in January 1837.

Francis Crump (No 1)

9 November 1741
Newcastle Street, near Fleet Market

14 May 1745
Newcastle Street, near Fleet Market

30 March 1748—9
Removed to Fenchurch Street

Removed to Nine Elms,
Battersea Parish,
20 July 1750

22 November 1753
with Gabriel Sleath
Gutter Lane

26 March 1756
Gutter Lane

17 October 1761
Gutter Lane, near Cheapside

He was the son of John Crump of Bewdley and was apprenticed to Gabriel Sleath on 30 August 1726. He obtained his freedom on 6 November 1741.

Another Francis Crump who was the son of Daniel Crump of Bewdley was apprenticed to Gabriel Sleath on 5 October 1752. He obtained his freedom on 6 May 1761. Possibly Francis Crump (No 1) was his uncle as they both originated from Bewdley. In the Parliamentary Return of 1773, a Francis Crump was entered as a Plateworker of Gutter Lane.

1 December 1703
Panton Street

1 December 1703
Panton Street

He obtained his freedom by Redemption on 1 December 1703 and was made a Liveryman in October 1708.

His son Samuel, was apprenticed to him and Daniel Shawe (Loriner) in 1710 and obtained his freedom in 1724.

D John Denziloe

27 October 1774
3 Westmoreland Buildings,
Aldersgate Street
Plate worker

He was not apprenticed through the Goldsmiths' Company
nor was he a Freeman of the Company.

Isaac Dighton

April 1697
Gutter Lane
Free Haberdasher

He was never a Freeman of the Goldsmiths' Company.

He was the son of Henry Dighton and was apprenticed to
William Browne, a member of the Haberdashers'
Company, on 26 May 1665. He obtained his freedom of
that Company on 7 June 1672.

Antony Nelme, who was apprenticed to Richard Rowley
in November 1672, was turned over to Isaac Dighton at
some later date during his apprenticeship.

19 March 1781
6 Albion Building, Aldersgate Street
Buckle maker

22 April 1784
3 Addle Street, Wood Street
Buckle maker

8 May 1786
3 Addle Street, Wood Street
Buckle maker

* 20 August 1801
3 Addle Street, Wood Street
Buckle maker

18 May 1813
30 Addle Street
Plate worker

5 March 1824
30 Addle Street

⊕ 18 October 1825
30 Addle Street

Removed to 16 Jewin Crescent,
Jewin Street, 20 December 1825

---

*   Mark entered in three sizes
⊕   Mark entered in two sizes

5 September 1828
16 Jewin Crescent, Jewin Street,
Plate worker

Removed to 2 Lovell's Court,
Paternoster Row, 31 December 1828

⊕ 31 December 1828
2 Lovell's Court, Paternoster Row
Plate worker

30 September 1830
2 Lovell's Court, Paternoster Row

27 January 1836
2 Lovell's Court, Paternoster Row

It would appear that these are the marks of two William
Eatons, probably father and son, who were Buckle maker
of 3 Addle Street and Plate worker of 30 Addle Street
respectively.

This assumption has been made since the signatures against
the marks of the Buckle maker were not written by the
same William Eaton as those against the Plate worker's.
Hence all those marks entered from 18 May 1813 onwards
are probably by William Eaton (No 2).

There is no record of either William Eaton being apprenticed through the Goldsmiths' Company or of them
becoming Freemen of the Company. On the other hand,
they may have been Freemen of one of the other City
Companies which further research may eventually disclose.

⊕ Mark entered in two sizes

31 December 1698
In Red Lion Court, Drury Lane
Free Draper

(No date. Probably entered 1720)
O.S.
Red Lion Court, Drury Lane.

He was the son of William Eckford (Blacksmith) and was apprenticed to Anthony Nelme (Goldsmith) on 11 September 1682.

This apprenticeship entry was scored out subsequently for some unknown reason and there is no record of his obtaining his freedom of the Goldsmiths' Company.

In the Goldsmiths' record book of marks he is noted as a Free Draper but again he has no freedom entry in the Drapers' Company records.

John Eckford (No 2)

20 June 1739
In the Inner Court, Red Cross Street

He was the son of John Eckford (No 1) and was apprenticed to John Fawdery on 24 January 1711. At a later date he was turned over to Philip Rollos and eventually obtained his freedom of the Goldsmiths' Company on 4 July 1723.

Edward Edwards

10 June 1811
with John Edwards

1 Bridgewater Square
Plate workers

19 September 1816
1 Bridgewater Square

Removed to 48 Banner Street, St Lukes, 5 March 1823.

Removed to 5 Radnor Street, St Lukes, 18 March 1825.

11 April 1828
42 Fetter Lane, Clerkenwell
Small worker

Removed to 60 Red Lion Street,
18 June 1829

 12 May 1840
(No address given)

 13 January 1841
(No address given)

He was the son of John Edwards and was apprenticed to
John Mewburn on 7 November 1797. He obtained his
freedom on 6 March 1811.

14 July 1824
with Henry and William Eley (No 2)
1 Lovell's Court, Paternoster Row
Plate workers

19 January 1825
2 Lovell's Court, Paternoster Row
Spoon maker

He was the son of William Eley (No 1) and was apprenticed to his father on 1 May 1811. He obtained his freedom of the Company on 4 November 1818 and presumably remained working with the family firm.

When his father died in 1824, he and his brothers (Henry and William No 2) entered a joint mark.

11 November 1777
with George Pierrepont
46 Little Bartholomew Close
Spoon makers

3 November 1778
4 New Street, Cloth Fair
Small worker

1 December 1778
2 George Street,
St Martins-le-Grand

29 April 1785
14 Clerkenwell Green
Buckle maker

12 March 1790
14 Clerkenwell Green

5 May 1795
14 Clerkenwell Green

4 January 1797
with William Fearn
14 Clerkenwell Green
Plate workers

29 January 1802
with William Fearn
1 Lovell's Court, Paternoster Row

18 April 1808
with William Fearn and William
Chawner (No 2)
1 Lovell's Court, Paternoster Row
Spoon makers

6 October 1814
with William Fearn
Lovell's Court, Paternoster Row
Spoon makers

14 May 1824
with William Fearn
1 Lovell's Court, Paternoster Row
Plate workers

He was the son of George Eley and was apprenticed to
William Fearn to learn the trade of goldsmith on 7
November 1770. He obtained his freedom on 4
November 1778, was made a Liveryman in October 1806
and died in 1824.

He had three sons, William (No 2), Charles and Henry,
who were apprenticed to him and became silversmiths.

14 July 1824
with Charles and Henry Eley
1 Lovell's Court, Paternoster Row
Plate workers

19 January 1825
3 Lovell's Court, Paternoster Row
Plate worker

22 June 1825
3 Lovell's Court

20 June 1826
3 Lovell's Court

5 December 1826
3 Lovell's Court

He was the son of William Eley (No 1) and was apprenticed to his father to learn the trade of silversmith on 3 February 1808. He obtained his freedom on 1 March 1815, was made a Liveryman in April 1816 and died in June 1841.

His two brothers, Charles and Henry, also became silversmiths. Charles was apprenticed to his father on 1 May 1811, obtained his freedom on 4 November 1818, and entered his own mark on 19 January 1825 from 2 Lovell's Court.

Henry was apprenticed to his father on 2 February 1814 and obtained his freedom on 6 February 1822.

27 August 1796
with Henry Chawner
Amen Corner
Plate workers

10 January 1798
Amen Corner
Plate worker

21 July 1802
Amen Corner

He was not apprenticed through the Goldsmiths' Company
nor was he a Freeman of the Company.

At the time of his joining Henry Chawner in partnership,
Edward Barnard was an employee in the workshop but
following Chawner's retirement, Barnard became leading
journeyman.

When John Emes died in 1808, his widow Rebecca,
took over the business.

30 June 1808
with William Emes
Amen Corner, Paternoster Row

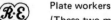

Plate workers

(These two marks were entered by
"Virtue of a Power of Attorney"
and signed by William Emes)

14 October 1808
with Edward Barnard
Amen Corner, Paternoster Row

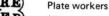

Plate workers

(These two marks were entered
by "Virtue of a Power of Attorney"
and signed by William Emes and
Edward Barnard).

20 February 1821
with Edward Barnard
Amen Corner, Paternoster Row

28 October 1825
with Edward Barnard
Amen Corner, Paternoster Row

She was the wife of John Emes and upon his death in 1808, took over the family business.

Her first mark was entered with a William Emes. His relationship to Rebecca is, as yet, unknown. Possibly he was a brother-in-law or a son.

This partnership did not last long for after two and a half months she took Edward Barnard, her husband's leading journeyman, into partnership.

This partnership continued until her death late in 1828.

Edward Barnard then brought his sons into the partnership and entered a joint mark in February 1829.

27 April 1813
18 Kings Head Court, Holborn Hill
Plate worker

20 May 1813
18 Kings Head Court, Holborn Hill

Removed to 24 Bridge Street,
Covent Garden 26 September 1818

17 March 1819
24 Bridges Street, Covent Garden
Plate worker

He was not apprenticed through the Goldsmiths' Company
nor was he a Freeman of the Company.

19 December 1743
St Swithins Lane

Presumably she was the wife of Thomas Farren and
entered her mark in 1743 upon his death.

Thomas Farren

 16 October 1707
Of St Swithins Lane

 15 June 1739
St Swithins Lane

He was the son of John Farren and was apprenticed to
William Denny on 8 April 1695. He obtained his freedom
on 3 October 1707, was made a Liveryman in 1721 and
an Assistant in 1731.

Presumably he died in 1743, when his wife Ann Farren
took over the business and entered her own mark.

John Pero was apprenticed to him in 1709 and obtained
his freedom in 1717.

Thomas Whipham was apprenticed to him in 1728 and
freed in 1737.

William Williams was apprenticed to him in 1731 and
freed in 1738.

28 September 1727
O.S.
Goldsmith Street, near Cheapside

She was the wife of William Fawdery and took over the business when her husband died in 1727.

John Fawdery (No 1 and 2)

April 1697
Foster Lane

27 February 1728—9
Hemings Row,
St Martin's Lane

John (No 1) was the son of John Fawdery and was apprenticed to Antony Nelme on 18 January 1687-8. He obtained his freedom on 11 September 1695 and was made a Liveryman in April 1705.

His brother was William Fawdery. His son John Fawdery (No 2) was apprenticed to Edward Cornock on 29 July 1718 but there is no record of his obtaining his freedom. This would not be necessary if he worked outside the city precincts.

The mark entered on 27 February 1728—9 is probably John Fawdery (No 2) as the address is outside the city.

April 1697

Goldsmith Street

28 July 1720
N.S.
Goldsmith Street

28 July 1720
O.S.
Goldsmith Street

He was the son of John Fawdery and was apprenticed to Robert Cooper on 15 December 1686. He obtained his freedom on 8 August 1694, was made a Liveryman in October 1708 and died in 1727. His wife Hester took over the business and entered her mark in September 1728.

His brother was John Fawdery (No 1).

April 1769
No 5 Brownlow Street,
Holborn

13 May 1774

75 Wood Street

Spoon maker

3 November 1786
with George Smith (No 3)
60 Paternoster Row
Plate workers
Removed to 1 Lovell's Court,
Paternoster Row, 29 June 1790.

4 January 1797
with William Eley (No 1)
14 Clerkenwell Green
Plate workers

29 January 1802
with William Eley (No 1)
1 Lovell's Court, Paternoster Row

18 April 1808
with William Eley (No 1) and
William Chawner (No 2)
1 Lovell's Court, Paternoster Row
Spoon makers

6 October 1814
with William Eley (No 1)

Lovell's Court, Paternoster Row
Spoon makers

14 May 1824
with William Eley (No 1)
1 Lovell's Court, Paternoster Row

Plate workers

He was the son of William Fearn and was apprenticed to
Thomas Chawner on 6 October 1762. He obtained his
freedom on 7 February 1770.
William Eley (No 1) was apprenticed to him in 1770.
William Chawner (No 2) was apprenticed to him in 1797.

25 September 1720
N.S.
Rose Street, Covent Garden

25 September 1720
O.S.
Rose Street, Covent Garden

15 June 1739
King Street, Covent Garden

He was the son of Peter Feline and was apprenticed to
Augustin Courtauld (No 1) on 31 March 1708—9. He
obtained his freedom on 6 April 1721, was made a
Liveryman in April 1731 and presumably died in
1753 when his wife Magdalen took over the business.

His son Edward, was apprenticed to him in 1745 and
eventually took up his freedom in 1763.

Fuller White was apprenticed to him in 1733 and
obtained his freedom in 1744.

15 May 1753
King Street, Covent Garden

18 January 1757
King Street, Covent Garden

She was the wife of Edward Feline and presumably she
took over the business when her husband died in 1753.
She appears to have continued working until 1762.

William Fleming F

April 1697
Of Cripplegate Without,
Maiden Lane

He was the son of John Fleming and was apprenticed to
Nathaniel Lock on 22 February 1687—8. He obtained
his freedom on 20 March 1694 and was made a Liveryman
in October 1708.

17 July 1780
with Stephen Gilbert
29 Church Street, St Anns
Plate workers

He was not apprenticed through the Goldsmiths' Company
nor was he a Freeman of the Company. He was of Swedish
origin. In the Parliamentary Return of 1773 he was
recorded as a Plateworker of Church Street, Soho.

Paul Storr was apprenticed to him about 1785 and
obtained his freedom in 1792.

Andrew Fogelberg probably retired in 1793 when Storr
took over his premises in Church Street.

3 February 1706 N.S.
St Swithins Lane

6 February 1720 O.S.
St Swithins Lane

He was the son of Thomas Folkington and was apprenticed
to John Bache on 9 March 1692—3. He obtained his
freedom on 23 June 1703 and was made a Liveryman in
October 1708.

Simon Jouet was apprenticed to him in 1717.

31 January 1706—7
Lombard Street
Free of the Wax Chandlers

He was never a Freeman of the Goldsmiths' Company.

He was the son of Richard Fordham and was apprenticed to Melior Benskin, widow of Richard Benskin, a member of the Wax Chandlers' Company, on 1 December 1686.

He obtained his freedom of that Company on 18 September 1693, was made a Liveryman in August 1694, a Steward in September 1705 and an Assistant in June 1710.

29 July 1791
with Daniel Pontifex
13 Hosier Lane, West Smithfield
Plate workers

1 September 1794
47 Red Lion Street, Clerkenwell
Plate worker

30 June 1798
47 Red Lion Street, Clerkenwell

5 February 1821
Harford Place, Huggerstone Bridge
Plate worker

He was the son of John Fountain and was apprenticed to
Fendall Rushforth and Daniel Smith (Merchant Taylor)
on 1 October 1777. He obtained his freedom on
2 February 1785.

F Charles Fox (No 1)

5 September 1804
139 Old Street, Goswell Street
Plate worker

He was not apprenticed through the Goldsmiths' Company nor was he a Freeman of the Company.

Apparently he entered only this mark, though it would appear that he was the founder of a firm which continued into the 1890's.

It is possible that his position as head of the firm was taken over in 1822 by his son Charles (No 2), although evidence suggests that he lived until about 1838.

F Charles Fox (No 2)

19 February 1822
139 Old Street
Plate worker

27 January 1823
139 Old Street

⊕ 21 August 1823
139 Old Street

23 September 1823
139 Old Street

⊕ Mark entered in two sizes

134

10 December 1823
139 Old Street

 9 May 1838
139 Old Street

He was not apprenticed through the Goldsmiths' Company nor was he a Freeman of the Company.

Apparently he assumed a leading position in his father's firm (Charles No 1) since his signature with the appendage "Junior" appears in the records beside all those marks entered in 1822 and 1823.

The same signature appears beside the 1838 entry but this time with the appendage "Senior". This would suggest that he had become head of the firm due to his father's death prior to this entry.

9 November 1729
with Joseph Allen
St Swithins Lane

21 August 1739
with Joseph Allen
St Swithins Lane

21 January 1746—47
St Swithins Lane

18 June 1755
St Swithins Lane

He was never a Freeman of the Goldsmiths' Company.

He was apprenticed to silversmith Francis Garthorne, a
member of the Girdlers' Company, on 2 October 1704
and became a Freeman of that Company on 15 July
1712.

17 January 1710—11
Maiden Lane, Covent Garden
Later moved to Lancaster Court
in the Strand

6 March 1722—3
Lancaster Court,
in the Strand

He was the son of Claude Fraillon and was apprenticed to
Philip Roker (No 1) on 25 April 1699. He obtained his
freedom on 1 March 1706.

He appears to have died in 1727 when his widow Blanche,
took over the business.

12 April 1791
with John Edwards
48 Jewin Street
Plate workers

11 January 1792
5 Cock Lane, Snowhill
Plate worker

2 May 1792 with Paul Storr
5 Cock Lane, Snowhill
Plate workers

23 June 1798
5 Cock Lane, Snowhill

2 June 1801
Inner Court, Bridewell Hospital
Plate worker

10 September 1811
with John Frisbee
Bridewell Hospital
Plate workers

 11 May 1814
with John Frisbee
Bridewell Hospital

He was the son of John Frisbee and was apprenticed to
John Crouch (No 1) to learn the trade of goldsmith on
5 October 1774. He obtained his freedom on 6 February
1782, was made Liveryman in October 1806 and died
on 9 December 1820.

His son John was apprenticed to him in 1799 and obtained
his freedom in 1806.

In 1811 and again in 1814, William entered a joint mark
with his son.

⊕ 29 December 1792
42 Monkwell Street
Plate worker

 ⊕ 11 July 1796
42 Monkwell Street
Removed to 3 Windsor Court,
Monkwell Street, 14 August 1797

 ⊕ 5 August 1823
(No address. Presumably at
Windsor Court)

He was not apprenticed through the Goldsmiths' Company
nor was he a Freeman of the Company.

⊕ Mark entered in two sizes.

12 June 1738
Gutter Lane
Free Goldsmith

23 June 1739
Gutter Lane

29 October 1743
Gutter Lane
 Mark entered due to the old
touchmark having broken

12 March 1743—44
Removed to St Paul's Churchyard

18 April 1751

28 April 1756

He was the son of John Garden and was apprenticed to
Gawen Nash on 4 February 1729-30. He obtained his
freedom on 3 October 1738, was made a Liveryman
in September 1746 and resigned on 9 December 1763.
He purchased some of Paul De Lamerie's patterns and
tools when auctioned, following Lamerie's death.

April 1697

In the Pall Mall

He was the son of Michel Garnier, a Huguenot refugee.
In 1687, he took out letters of denization, then obtained
his freedom by Redemption on 29 May 1696 by order
of the Court of Aldermen.
In October 1698 he was made a Liveryman.
He was related to Jean Chartier's wife, Suzanne Garnier;
possibly her brother.

Robert Garrard

20 October 1792
with John Wakelin
Panton Street
Plate workers

11 August 1802
Panton Street, Haymarket
Plate worker

18 April 1818
Panton Street

(Note that an Old English E was used
in this mark in mistake for a G.)

17 January 1822
Panton Street, St Martins
Removed to 29 Panton Street,
27 February 1836.

29 June 1847

29 Panton Street

He was the second son of Robert Hazelfoot Garrard and
Miriam Richards. His father, who was a Linen draper in
Cheapside, died on 29 March 1785. His mother died in
1801.

Robert was baptized in December 1758 and apprenticed
in 1773 to Steven Unwin, a hardwareman of Cheapside,
who was a Freeman of the Grocers' Company. Thus
Robert obtained his freedom of the Grocers' Company by
service in 1780. He was made a Liveryman of the Company
in 1818 and later became its Master.

Soon after obtaining his freedom, he joined the firm of
Wakelin & Co., goldsmiths of Panton Street. Presumably
he was on the retail side as he never had any training as a
goldsmith. He appears to have become a partner in 1792
when he entered his first mark in partnership with John
Wakelin.

Eventually he was in complete control of the firm, so that
in 1802 he entered his own mark.

One of his sons, James, obtained his freedom of the
Goldsmiths' Company by Redemption in June 1825, was
made a Liveryman in 1829, Assistant in 1842 and
eventually Prime Warden in 1847 and 1850. He died in
1870.

143

April 1697
St Swithins Lane
Free Girdler

He was never a Freeman of the Goldsmiths' Company.

Apparently he obtained his freedom of the Girdlers'
Company at some date prior to 1694, this being as far
back as existing Freedom records reach.

In 1718 he became Master of the Girlders' Company, which
was the equivalent of Prime Warden of the Goldsmiths'
Company.

His son, Robert, having been apprenticed to him, obtained
his freedom of the Girdlers' Company on 15 July 1712.

Mordecai Fox was also apprenticed to Francis Garthorne
and obtained his freedom of the Girdlers' Company on
the same day in 1712. Fox later entered into partnership
with the silversmith Joseph Allen.

Silversmith George Garthorne was apprenticed to a
Francis Garthorne in 1669, but it is unlikely that this
was the same Francis as noted here.

Possibly the two Francis Garthornes were father and son.

April 1697
Keyre Lane

He was the son of John Garthorne and was apprenticed to
Thomas Payne and Francis Garthorne on 18 August 1669.
He obtained his freedom on 11 August 1680.

Presumably he was a relation of this particular Francis
Garthorne.

Benjamin Gignac

28 February 1744—45
Deans Court, St Martins-le-Grand

He was not apprenticed through the Goldsmiths' Company
nor was he a Freeman of the Company.

His address of St Martins-le-Grand, although within the
city, was known as a "liberty" area which meant it had
been exempt from the city's civil laws. Because of this
he was not obliged to be a Freeman while working in
'this locality.

In the Parliamentary Return of 1773 he was recorded as
a Plateworker of Deans Court, St Martins-le-Grand

17 July 1780
with Andrew Fogelberg
29 Church Street, St Anns
Plate workers

He was the son of John Gilbert and was apprenticed to
Edward Wakelin on 8 May 1752. He obtained his
freedom on 1 February 1764.

He returned to work for John Parker and Edward
Wakelin at Panton Street from 1766 to 1771.

In 1780 he joined the Swedish silversmith, Andrew
Fogelberg, as his partner.

20 November 1754
Wardour Street

15 June 1782
25 Queen Street, Seven Dials
Plate worker

He was not apprenticed through the Goldsmiths' Company,
nor was he a Freeman of the Company.

In the Parliamentary Return of 1773 he was recorded as a
Plateworker of Wardour Street, Soho.

It is possible that the second entry of 15 June 1782 is that
of his son Pierre (No 2), but as yet no information has come
to light to confirm this point.

Thomas Gilpin

2 July 1739
Lincolns Inn,
Bargate

Thomas was possibly the son of Robert Gilpin, he being
the only Thomas in the Goldsmiths' freedom and
apprenticeship records for that period. If this is correct
he was apprenticed to John Wells on 7 January 1718—19.
There is no record of his having obtained his freedom but
this would not be necessary working outside the city
precincts.

20 November 1784
86 Cheapside
Plate worker

27 November 1784

86 Cheapside

13 September 1786
with Edward Wigan
86 Cheapside,
Plate workers

14 August 1787
with Edward Wigan
86 Cheapside

26 July 1792
with Edward Wigan
86 Cheapside

15 March 1800
with Edward Wigan and James Bult
(No address)
Plate workers

16 September 1818
with James Bult
86 Cheapside
Plate workers

He was not apprenticed through the Goldsmiths' Company
nor was he a Freeman of the Company.

He appears to have retired or died in 1819 as James Bult
entered his own mark on 13 July 1819.

G Benjamin Godfrey

18 June 1739

Norris Street in St James, Haymarket

Goldsmith

He was not apprenticed through the Goldsmiths' Company nor was he a Freeman of the Company.

About 1734 he married Elizabeth Buteux, widow of Abraham Buteux.

In 1741 Benjamin Godfrey died and Elizabeth, now widowed for a second time, took over the business and entered her own mark yet again.

Elizabeth Godfrey

29 June 1741

Norris Street in St James, Haymarket

She was the widow of Abraham Buteux and about 1734 married Benjamin Godfrey.

When Benjamin died in 1741 she took over the family business and entered her own mark.

She appears to have continued working until circa 1755.

N.B. For her previous mark, look under Elizabeth Buteux.

N.S.   19 November 1722

At the Three Golden Lions
in Gutter Lane

O.S.   Free of the Goldsmiths'
Company

(No date. Between October 1732
and July 1734).

At the Three Golden Lions
in Gutter Lane

Removed out of Gutter Lane to
the Golden Bottle in Ave Maria Lane,
25 March 1741

31 August 1747
(No address.
Presumably Ave Maria Lane)

He was the son of James Gould and was apprenticed to
David Green on 26 October 1714. He obtained his freedom of the Goldsmiths' Company on 8 November 1722,
was made a Liveryman in 1739 and an Assistant of the
Company in 1745.

His brother William, was apprenticed to him in January
1723—24.

John Cafe was apprenticed to him in 1730.

20 October 1732
At the Wheatsheaf
in Gutter Lane

24 July 1734
At the Candlestick
in Foster Lane

He was the son of James Gould and was apprenticed to
his brother James, on 9 January 1723—24. He obtained
his freedom of the Goldsmiths' Company on 5 April
1733, was made a Liveryman in September 1746 and
resigned on 14 December 1763.

23 December 1743
Fetter Lane

24 June 1748
Pemberton Row, Goff Square

30 June 1748
Pemberton Row, Goff Square

26 May 1754
Removed to Fetter Lane

20 September 1777
Fetter Lane
Plate worker

23 February 1779
with Edward Fernell

119 Fetter Lane

He was the son of Charles Grundy and was apprenticed to
Edward Vincent on 2 April 1731. He obtained his
freedom on 6 February 1738 and was made a Liveryman
in January 1750.

5 January 1716—17

At the Mitre in the Strand

He was the son of John Guerrier and was apprenticed to
Pierre Harache (No 2) on 26 September 1700. He obtained
his freedom on 24 December 1716.

19 October 1727
with Thomas Cooke
At the Golden Cup,
Foster Lane

23 December 1734
with Thomas Cooke
At the Golden Cup,
Foster Lane

28 June 1739
with Thomas Cooke
Foster Lane

17 February 1748—49
with Thomas Cooke
Foster Lane

30 July 1750
with Thomas Cooke
Foster Lane

He was the son of George Gurney and was apprenticed to
Richard Bayley on 2 May 1717. He obtained his freedom
on 3 September 1724, was made a Liveryman in 1736 and
an Assistant in 1752. He became 4th Warden in 1763, 3rd
Warden in 1764 and 2nd Warden in 1765.

William Priest was apprenticed to him in 1740.

18 March 1735—36
Great Newport Street,
near Long Acre

4 August 1738
Church Street, St Anns,
Soho

20 June 1739
Church Street, St Ann, Soho
Goldsmith

He was not apprenticed through the Goldsmiths' Company
nor was he a Freeman of the Company.

7 March 1715—16
Great St Andrews Street
in St Giles
Free Longbow string maker

24 May 1721
(No address given but probably
was Great St Andrews Street)

He was not apprenticed through the Goldsmiths' Company
nor was he a Freeman of the Company.

He was a Freeman of the Longbow String Makers'
Company having obtained his freedom by Redemption on
7 March 1715.

He appears to have been 2nd Warden or Lower Warden in
1726—7 and Prime Warden or Upper Warden in 1727—8.
He was an Assistant of the Court in 1731, 1732 and 1733
and may have been so for further years but unfortunately
the Accounts records for 1734 onwards appear to have
been lost or destroyed.

Circa
1767

These two marks are not
recorded at Goldsmiths' Hall.
They are assumed to be
J. Crouch and T. Hannam
and possibly entered in the
missing volumes

Circa
1773

13 April 1799
with John Crouch
37 Monkwell Street
Plate workers

He was the son of William Hannam and was apprenticed
to John Cafe on 6 November 1754.

He was turned over to William Cafe by consent of John's
executor on 13 October 1757.

He obtained his freedom on 2 December 1761.

16 February 1737–8
Seven Dials in Great St Andrew Street,
at Blackmoors Head, St Giles
Silversmith

He was not apprenticed through the Goldsmiths' Company
nor was he a Freeman of the Company.

Presumably he was related to Pierre Harache (No 2).

Jean Harache

22 June 1726
Ryders Court, St Anns parish
Foreigner

He was not apprenticed through the Goldsmiths' Company
nor was he a Freeman of the Company.

Presumably he was related to Pierre Harache (No 2).

April 1697
Suffolk Street,
nearing Charing Cross

He was a Huguenot immigrant from France.
He obtained his freedom by Redemption on 21 July 1682
by order of a Court of Aldermen and was made a Liveryman in November 1687.
Simon Pantin (No 1) was apprenticed to him and obtained
his freedom in 1701.
His son was Pierre Harache (No 2).

Pierre Harache (No 2)

25 October 1698
Compton Street,
near St Anns' Church,
Soho

He was the son of Pierre Harache (No 1) and obtained his
freedom by Redemption on 24 October 1698 by order of
a Court of Aldermen.
John Peter Guerrier was apprenticed to him in 1700.

+ 14 November 1808
13 Clerkenwell Close
Large worker

    22 February 1810
with Thomas Wallis
16 Red Lion Street, Clerkenwell
Plate workers

 * 3 December 1817
with Thomas Wallis
16 Red Lion Street

    17 February 1820
with Thomas Wallis
16 Red Lion Street

 * 3 July 1821
Red Lion Square, Clerkenwell
Plate worker

 ⊕ 19 June 1823
Red Lion Square

    29 October 1829
Red Lion Square

⊕ Mark entered in two sizes
* Mark entered in three sizes
+ Mark entered in four sizes

* 12 April 1832
  Red Lion Square

* 13 May 1834
  Red Lion Square

He was the son of Jonathan Hayne (surgeon) of Red Lion Street, Clerkenwell who had died before he was apprenticed on 1 June 1796 to Thomas Wallis (Goldsmith), also of Red Lion Street.

Presumably the death of Jonathan's father left the family in financial difficulties since the £5 apprenticeship fee due to Wallis was paid by the charity of the Governors of Christ's Hospital, London. On the 4 January 1804, the Governors paid a similar fee for Jonathan's brother, Samuel Holditch John, to be apprenticed likewise to Wallis.

Jonathan obtained his freedom of the Goldsmiths' Company on 4 January 1804, (the same day as his brother's apprenticeship began), was made a Liveryman in 1811 and an Assistant in 1836. He became 4th Warden in 1840, 3rd Warden in 1841, 2nd Warden in 1842 and Prime Warden in 1843. He died in 1848.

He had two sons who became Freemen of the Company by Patrimony, Samuel Holditch Thomas (Silversmith of Red Lion Street) on 1 April 1835 and Watson Ward (Gentleman of Croydon, Surrey) on 6 December 1843.

* Mark entered in three sizes.

Samuel, who was made a Liveryman in 1839 and an
Assistant in 1850, resigned from the Company in 1854
and died on 4 August 1887. Watson, who was made a
Liveryman in February 1847, died on 15 June 1893.

Thomas Hayter   H

7 January 1792
with George Smith (No 5)
4 Higgin Lane
Plate workers

21 May 1805
4 Huggin Lane, Wood Street
Plate worker

15 March 1816
with George Hayter
Huggin Alley, Wood Street
Plate workers

7 December 1821
with George Hayter
Huggin Alley
Wood Street

163

He was the son of John Hayter and was apprenticed to
George Smith (No 5) to learn the trade of silversmith on
4 December 1782. He obtained his freedom on 3 February
1790, was made a Liveryman in October 1801 and died
on 2 September 1840.
His son and partner, George Smith Hayter,
obtained his freedom of the Goldsmiths' Company
by Patrimony on 7 December 1814, was made
a Liveryman in 1816 and an Assistant in 1846.
He twice held the position of Prime Warden, in
1854 and again in 1863.

George Heming

17 November 1774
with William Chawner (No 1)
Bond Street
Plate workers

15 February 1781
with William Chawner (No. 1)

Old Bond Street

He was the son of Thomas Heming and was apprenticed to
his father on 2 March 1763. There is no record of his having
obtained his freedom but this would not be obligatory as his
address was outside the city precincts.

When his partnership with William Chawner (No. 1)
terminated circa 1790–1, he continued running the
business at 151 New Bond Street. In 1794 a Richard
Heming was at this address. Possibly he was a son.

12 June 1745
Piccadilly

Circa
1770

This mark is not recorded at
Goldsmiths' Hall. Is assumed
to be Thomas Heming and
possibly was entered in one
of the missing volumes.

He was the son of Richard Heming and was apprenticed to
Edmund Boddington on 7 February 1737—8. On the same
day he was turned over to Peter Archambo (No 1). He
obtained his freedom on 7 May 1746, was made a Liveryman in June 1763 and died between 1795 and 1801.

His sons were George Heming who was apprenticed to him
in 1763 and Thomas Heming who was apprenticed to him
in 1767. There is no record of either son obtaining his
freedom but this was not obligatory as they were outside
the city precincts.

23 June 1736
Kings Head Court,
Gutter Lane

Circa
1739

These two marks are not in the
records at Goldsmiths' Hall.
As the marks have been
virtually proven from other
sources, they are presumed

Circa
1756

to have been entered in the
missing volumes

9 June 1763
with Robert Hennell (No 1)
Foster Lane

9 July 1768
with Robert Hennell (No 1)
Foster Lane

He was the son of Robert Hennell, a framework knitter of Newport Pagnell, Buckinghamshire, who founded a drapery business and later, in 1707, became vicar of Newport Pagnell church.

David, born on 8 December 1712, was sent to London and apprenticed to Edward Wood on 6 September 1728. He obtained his freedom on 4 December 1735 and in June 1736 set up in business under the sign of the "Fleur-de-Lis and Star" in Gutter Lane.

William Hennell his half brother was apprenticed to him on 7 April 1737 and obtained his freedom on 12 June 1745. He probably remained working for the firm.

David's wife had fifteen children; nine died before they were one year old and of four sons called David, only one survived his father. One son, John, obtained his freedom by Patrimony on 3 June 1772 but did not take up the Goldsmith's trade. Another son, Robert (No 1) was born in 1741 and apprenticed to David in 1756. He obtained his freedom on 8 June 1763 and the following day entered a joint mark in partnership with his father.

David was made a Liveryman in June 1763 and a Deputy or Touch Warden in 1773. About this time he retired leaving Robert (No 1) to carry on the family business.

David eventually died in 1785.

15 July 1795
with Robert Hennell (No 1)
11 Foster Lane
Plate workers

5 January 1802
with Robert Hennell (No 1)
& Samuel Hennell
11 Foster Lane
Plate workers

He was the son of Robert Hennell (No 1) and was born in 1767. He was apprenticed to his father on 6 February 1782 and obtained his freedom on 5 August 1789.

His two brothers, Robert and Samuel were also apprenticed to their father.

Samuel obtained his freedom in 1800 but there is no record of Robert having completed his apprenticeship.

In February 1791, David was made a Liveryman and in 1795 he and his father entered their joint mark. In 1802 they entered another mark including Samuel in the partnership. Later that year, David appears to have retired from the firm when Samuel and his father entered their own mark.

David resigned his position of Liveryman in the Goldsmiths' Company on 4 December 1821.

9 June 1763
with David Hennell (No 1)
Foster Lane

9 July 1768
with David Hennell (No 1)
Foster Lane

30 May 1772
Foster Lane

9 October 1773
16 Foster Lane
Salt maker

15 July 1795
with David Hennell (No 2)
11 Foster Lane
Plate workers

5 January 1802
with David Hennell (No 2)
& Samuel Hennell
11 Foster Lane
Plate workers

28 October 1802
with Samuel Hennell
11 Foster Lane
Plate workers

He was the son of David Hennell (No 1) and was born in 1741. He was one of fifteen children of whom only five reached maturity, nine having died before they were one year old.

He was apprenticed to his father on 5 April 1756 and obtained his freedom on 8 June 1763. The following day he entered his first partnership mark with his father.

He was made a Liveryman in July 1763 and when his father retired in 1772, he took over the business and entered his own mark.

His nephew, Robert Hennell (No 2), son of brother John, was apprenticed to him on 8 April 1778 and later founded his own firm.

Robert (No 1) had three sons, David (No 2), Robert and Samuel who were apprenticed to him. Samuel eventually took over the family business when Robert (No 1) died in 1811.

17 June 1808
with Henry Nutting
38 Noble Street, Foster Lane
Plate workers

3 November 1809
35 Noble Street, Foster Lane
Plate worker
Removed to 3 Lancaster Court,
Strand 28 June 1817.

11 August 1820
3 Lancaster Court, Strand

23 January 1826
3 Lancaster Court, Strand
Removed to 14 Northumberland Street,
Strand 14 January 1828

Born in 1769, he was the son of John Hennell and nephew of Robert Hennell (No 1).

John Hennell had obtained his freedom by Patrimony in 1772 but instead of entering the Goldsmiths' trade, he made a living out of his grandfather's drapery business at Newport Pagnell.

Robert (No 2), therefore, was apprenticed to his uncle Robert (No 1) on 8 April 1778 and two days later to John Houle, an engraver. Both apprenticeships were to run concurrently.

He obtained his freedom on 1 June 1785 and then moved to Windmill Court, Smithfield where he probably worked only at engraving. He did not enter his own mark until 1808 when he went into partnership with Henry Nutting as the senior partner. In 1809 Robert moved from No 38 to No 35 Noble Street where he set up on his own.

When he eventually retired on 25 May 1834, his son Robert (No 3) took over the family business.

Robert (No 3) had been born in 1794 and obtained his freedom by Patrimony in 1834.

5 January 1802
with Robert Hennell (No 1)
& David Hennell (No 2)

11 Foster Lane

Plate workers

28 October 1802
with Robert Hennell (No 1)
11 Foster Lane
Plate workers

22 June 1811
11 Foster Lane
Plate worker

6 April 1814
with John Terry
Foster Lane
Plate workers

27 July 1816
8 Aldermanbury
(This is a re-entry of the same mark
entered on 22 June 1811)

Removed to 8 Charles Street,
Goswell Street, 19 September 1816

Removed to 11 Foster Lane,
7 August 1817

Removed to 5 Snowhill,
18 May 1818

He was the son of Robert Hennell (No 1) and was born in 1778. Although apprenticed to his father, he obtained his freedom by Patrimony on 2 December 1800.

His two elder brothers David (No 2) and Robert were also apprenticed to their father but only David obtained his freedom.

In 1802, Samuel joined his father and brother David in entering their joint mark. Later that year, Samuel and his father entered another mark, presumably because David had retired from the firm. When Robert (No 1) died in 1811, Samuel took over the business.

In 1814, Samuel formed a partnership with John Terry who had married one of his nieces. After two years, Samuel returned to working on his own. He eventually died in 1837.

Samuel's eldest son, another Samuel, did not serve any apprenticeship and his second son, Robert George, became a jeweller in Holborn.

11 May 1731
with Robert Abercromby

Christophers Court
St Martins-le-Grand

6 July 1731

Christophers Court
St Martins-le-Grand

(No entry date. Entry made between
preceeding maker's mark of 24 December
1735 and following maker's mark of
18 March 1736)

Glasshouse Yard,
Blackfriars

27 June 1739

Glasshouse Yard, Blackfriars

Removed to Essex Street,
in the Strand, 7 December 1748

Removed to the Strand, 9 July 1753

15 September 1753

He was not apprenticed through the Goldsmiths' Company
nor was he a Freeman of the Company.

H Edward Holaday

 1 November 1709
Grafton Street

He was the son of Edward Holaday and was apprenticed
to John Bache on 22 December 1699. He obtained his
freedom on 14 September 1709, was made a Liveryman
in December 1717 and died in June 1719.

His wife was Sarah Holaday who carried on the business
after his death.

H Sarah Holaday

 22 July 1719
Grafton Street

 15 June 1725
O.S.
Grafton Street

She was the wife of Edward Holaday and took over the
business when he died in 1719.

3 August 1703
Horse-shoe Alley,
Crunhill Fields

He was the son of Edmund Holliday and was apprenticed
to Benjamin Nelson on 25 February 1690—91.

He was turned over to Thomas Elton at a later date and
eventually obtained his freedom on 8 July 1703.

7 October 1724
O.S.
At the Crown, Noble Street

7 January 1724—5
N.S.
At the Crown, Noble Street

15 May 1734
At the Hat and Feather,
Goswell Street

21 January 1739—40
Goswell Street

He was the son of Samuel Hutton and was apprenticed to
Edward Jennings on 4 April 1717. He obtained his
freedom on 7 May 1724.

Possibly he died in 1740 when Sarah Hutton, who
presumably was his wife, entered her own mark.

His son, Charles, obtained his freedom by Patrimony on
7 May 1760.

Thomas Northcote was apprenticed to Charles Hutton and
Thomas Chawner in 1763.

20 June 1740
Goswell Street
Free Goldsmith
Removed to Noble Street near
Goswell Street 15 March 1747

She was probably the wife of Samuel Hutton, and entered
her mark when he retired or died in 1740.

She was a Freeman of the Goldsmiths' Company and
apparently obtained it by Patrimony on 7 April 1737
when still Sarah Penkethman before her marriage to
Samuel Hutton.

HH 12 April 1821
5 Castle Street, Houndsditch
Plate worker

HH 23 May 1821
5 Castle Street

HH
HH 29 June 1821
5 Castle Street

HH 5 October 1821
5 Castle Street

HH
HH 6 October 1821
5 Castle Street

He was not apprenticed through the Goldsmiths' Company
nor was he a Freeman of the Company.

26 January 1741
Little Brittain

24 September 1757
with Charles Semore

Deans Court,
St Martins-le-Grand

(As the original of this mark in the
Goldsmiths' records is very blurred
indeed, it is impossible to decipher the
shape of the central symbol. Because of
this, it is illustrated here as a dot only.)

Removed to Noble Street,
24 October 1758.

He was the son of John Hyatt and was apprenticed to
James Gould on 10 May 1733. He obtained his freedom
on 5 March 1740.

April 1697
Fleet Street

He was the son of William Jackson and was apprenticed to Richard Bransfield on 10 October 1674 and later turned over to John Spakeman or Spackman.

He obtained his freedom on 23 December 1681.

3 May 1734
Hemings Row
near St Martins Lane

20 June 1739
Hemings Row

7 July 1760

Removed to Spur Street,
Leicester Field

He was not apprenticed through the Goldsmiths' Company,
nor was he a Freeman of the Company. This would not be
necessary as he was working outside the city precincts.

In 1738, he married Anne Courtauld, the sister of Samuel
Courtauld (No 1). They had several children. One of them
was Judith, born 1741, who married goldsmith George
Cowles in 1768.

George Cowles had served his apprenticeship under
Samuel Courtauld (No 1).

23 November 1723

Over against ye Victualling Office,
Little Tower Hill

He was not apprenticed through the Goldsmiths' Company,
nor was he a Freeman of the Company. Prior to coming
to London, he traded as a silversmith in the town of
Exeter.

Peter probably retired or died in 1725 when his son Simon
took over the premises and entered a new mark.

Simon Jouet

(No date given. Presumably entered
between May and July 1725.)

N.S.

Maiden Lane

21 July 1725

O.S.

Over against ye Victualling Office,
Little Tower Hill

Circa
1726

This mark is not recorded at
Goldsmiths' Hall. Presumed to be
Simon Jouet but not entered due to
its similarity with the previous mark.

18 June 1739

At the White Heart, Foster Lane

Removed to Carey Lane
9 September 1746

29 February 1747—48

Now at Aldersgate, Within
5 April 1748

Removed to Kingsland
27 March 1755

He was the son of Peter Jouet and was apprenticed to John
Orchard and Thomas Folkingham on 3 April 1718. He
obtained his freedom on 27 May 1725 and entered his
second mark in July when he appears to have taken over
his father's premises.

William Cafe was turned over to him in 1746 having been
apprenticed to John Cafe in 1741.

29 August 1727
N.S..
with James Murray
St Martin's Lane

29 August 1727
O.S.
with James Murray
St Martin's Lane

29 August 1727
N.S.

St Martin's Lane

29 August 1727
O.S.

St Martin's Lane

Of German origin, he was not apprenticed through the
Goldsmiths' Company nor was he a Freeman of the
Company.

Evidently he was a relation of Charles Frederick Kandler,
possibly his father, since Frederick used Charles' last
new standard mark for his own in 1735. This probably
occurred following Charles' death.

A similar example of this occurrence was Francis Nelme
using his father's marks in 1722—23.

However, it is thought possible that Charles (No 1) and
Charles Frederick may have been the same person although
this would mean he had worked for about fifty years,
unusual at that time.

12 November 1778
100 Jermyn Street
Plate worker

He was not apprenticed through the Goldsmiths' Company nor was he a Freeman of the Company.

Probably he was the son of Frederick Kandler as they were of the same address, namely Jermyn Street.

Charles' entry of 1778 was probably due to the death or retirement of Frederick Kandler.

10 September 1735
N.S.

10 September 1735
O.S.

German Street,
near St James Church

25 June 1739
Harman Street

24 June 1758
Harman Street

He was not a Freeman of the Goldsmiths' Company. He was evidently a relation of Charles Kandler (No 1), possibly his son, as he took Charles' new standard mark for his own in 1735. Presumably Charles died at this time.

In the Parliamentary Return of 1773, Frederick was recorded as a plate worker of Jermyn Street.

His son was probably Charles Kandler (No 2) who entered his mark in 1778 from the same address due to the death or retirement of Frederick.

16 June 1747
Foster Lane

She was the wife of Richard Kersill and took over the family business in 1747 when her husband died.

Richard Kersill

20 April 1744
Foster Lane

He was the son of William Kersill (Maltster) and was apprenticed to George Greenhill Jones on 1 July 1736.

He obtained his freedom on 7 February 1743.

When he died in 1747, his wife Ann, took over the family business.

His brother Thomas, was apprenticed to Walter Brind in 1749 and obtained his freedom in 1757.

21 August 1749
Gutter Lane

 2 July 1757
Gutter Lane

He was not apprenticed through the Goldsmiths' Company
nor was he a Freeman of the Company. Possibly he was
a Freeman of another Company.

18 June 1739
Foster Lane

26 January 1742—43
Due to the old mark being broken

14 February 1743—44
Due to the old mark being broken

He was not apprenticed through the Goldsmiths' Company
nor was he a Freeman of the Company.
Possibly he was a Freeman of another Company.

1698
Sherborne Lane

He was the son of John Ladyman (Salter) and was apprenticed to George Watkins (Goldsmith) on 2 July 1675.

He obtained his freedom on 28 September 1687 and was made a Liveryman in October 1698.

Thomas Sutton was apprenticed to him in 1702.

George Lambe

10 June 1713
Hemings Row
St Martin's Lane

He was the son of William Lambe and was apprenticed to Joseph Barbutt on 23 May 1706. He obtained his freedom on 10 June 1713 and presumably died in 1719 when his wife, Jane, entered her widow's mark.

His son, Edward John, was apprenticed to Jane Lambe on 2 April 1730 and obtained his freedom by Patrimony on 3 February 1742.

(No month) 1719—20
N.S.
Chandos Street

(No month) 1719—20
O.S.
Chandos Street

She was the wife of George Lambe and presumably took over the business when her husband died in 1719.

Their son, Edward John, was apprenticed to her in 1730 and obtained his freedom by Patrimony in 1742.

Jonathan Lambe

1697
On London Bridge

He was the son of John Lambe (Clerk) and was apprenticed to Richard Connyers (Goldsmith) on 26 March 1690.

He obtained his freedom of the Goldsmiths' Company on 1 July 1697.

5 February 1711—12
N.S.

Windmill Street,
near the Haymarket

    This mark is not recorded at
Circa Goldsmiths' Hall.
1717 Presumed to be
    Paul De Lamerie

17 March 1732
O.S.

At the Golden Ball,
Windmill Street,
St James

27 June 1739
Gerrard Street

He was the son of Paul Souchay de la Merie and
Constance le Roux, both French Huguenots of aristocratic
birth. They had fled to the Netherlands to escape from
the religious persecution that followed the repeal of the
Edict of Nantes by Louis XIV on 24 October 1685.
Young Paul was born in the Netherlands at Bois-le-Duc or
Hertogenbosch, this being its Dutch name, on 9 April
1688 and was baptised Paul Jacques at the local church
on 14 April 1688.

In 1691 his parents brought him to London where they
lived in a small house in Berwick Street, Soho.

His father was not trained for any trade or profession, so probably their only income at times was a small pension from the Royal Bounty, a fund for assisting distressed Huguenot refugees. In 1703, this pension amounted to £6 for the year. Later, when young Paul was established in his own business, his mother came to live with him until her death in 1741, but for some reason his father and he were so estranged that he allowed him to become an inmate of the poor house where he died and had a pauper's funeral in 1735. On 7 July 1703 young Paul took out letters of denization and on 6 August of that year he was apprenticed to the Huguenot silversmith, Pierre Platel. On 4 February 1712 he obtained his freedom and the following day entered his first mark at the Goldsmiths' Hall.

In 1717 he was made a Liveryman of the Goldsmiths' Company and in 1731 an Assistant of the Court.

On 11 February 1717 he married 23 year old Louise Julliot, the daughter of a Huguenot family. They had six children of whom three died in childhood. They were Margaret born 1718, died 1724; Paul born 1725, died 1727; and Daniel born 1727, died 1728. The three remaining children were Susan born 1720; Susannah born 1729 and Louisa born 1730. Susannah married Joseph Debaufre of the watch making family in 1750 and Susan married one John Malliet in 1754, but Louisa remained a spinster until her death in 1761.

Apparently Paul belonged to a militia organisation of some kind, for in 1736 he became a Captain and from 1743 was a Major until his death in 1751.

He became 4th Warden of the Goldsmiths' Company in 1743, 3rd Warden in 1746 and 2nd Warden in 1747. During 1750, his health began to fail and he eventually died at his home in Gerrard Street on 1 August 1751.

As he had no son or heir to take over the business, he directed in his will that the business be closed and all plate in hand be completed and sold.

Peter Archambo (No 2) was apprenticed to him in 1738 and obtained his freedom in 1748.

John Lampfert

12 November 1748
Little Windmill Street

21 January 1748-9
Little Windmill Street

Removed to Hemings Row
24 November 1749

He was not apprenticed through the Goldsmiths' Company nor was he a Freeman of the Company.

3 March 1780
with John Robertson

Plate workers at
Newcastle-upon-Tyne

(These marks were entered
at the Goldsmiths' Hall
"by virtue of a letter of
Attorney")

He was apprenticed to Isaac Cookson, a Newcastle silversmith, on 2 October 1731. After completing his apprenticeship, he remained with Cookson as one of his journeymen.
When Cookson died in August 1754, he entered into
partnership with fellow journeyman John Goodrick. Both
he and Goodrick obtained their freedom of the Goldsmiths'
Company of Newcastle on 24 September 1754.

In April 1757, Goodrick died leaving Langlands to continue
running the business on his own.

In 1778, he took John Robertson into partnership which
lasted until Langland's death on 10 April 1793.

His wife then continued the partnership with Robertson
presumably until her son, John Langlands (No 2), became
free by Patrimony on 24 December 1793.

On 10 June 1795, the partnership was dissolved and on
11 July 1795 John Langlands (No 2) set up in business on
his own. He died on 9 May 1804 when only 31 years old
leaving his widow, Dorothy, to continue the firm.

N.B.   Presumably these three marks above were
      entered in the London Goldsmiths'
      records for use on articles made for the
      London market. The firm's premises
      remained at Newcastle-upon-Tyne
      throughout this period.

19 November 1725
"Lomber Cow" at corner of
Seven Dials

31 July 1739
Lomber Court,
by Seven Dials

He was not apprenticed through the Goldsmiths' Company
nor was he a Freeman of the Company.

In June 1742, he and five other goldsmiths were charged
with counterfeiting assay marks on wrought plate to avoid
paying duty and assay charges. By August 1742, he had
been prosecuted, tried and convicted of the charge and
was then residing in the Kings Bench Prison.

The other five goldsmiths so charged were:-

Richard Gosling, Edward Aldridge, James Smith, David
Mowden and Matthias Standfast.

13 July 1711
Castle Street
near Hemings Row

12 December 1721
O.S.
(No address. Presumably as above)

He was the son of Joseph Lea (Yeoman) and was
apprenticed to John Diggle (Goldsmith) on 8 June 1698.
He obtained his freedom of the Goldsmiths' Company
on 13 July 1709.

Ralph Leake

April 1697
Covent Garden

He was the son of Thomas Leake and was apprenticed to
Thomas Littleton on 15 July 1664. He obtained his
freedom on 20 September 1671, was made an Assistant
in 1703 and 4th Warden in 1714.

L **Samuel Lee**

14 August 1701
Newgate Street

1 July 1720
O.S.
(No address. Presumably as above)

He was the son of George Lee (Grocer) and was apprenticed to William Swadling (Goldsmith) on 9 September 1692. At a later date he was turned over to John Penford and later again turned over to John Archbold. He eventually obtained his freedom of the Goldsmiths' Company on 7 August 1701.

John Leech

April 1697
Distaff Lane

He was not apprenticed through the Goldsmiths' Company nor was he a Freeman of the Company.

9 June 1760
Porter Street, Seven Dials

ILI 5 February 1773
Litchfield Street, Soho

He was not apprenticed through the Goldsmiths' Company
nor was he a Freeman of the Company.

8 November 1791
15 Great Sutton Street
Buckle maker

29 September 1792
with Dennis Charie
16 Albemarle Street, St Johns Lane
Buckle maker

3 July 1794
Removed to 13 Bethnal Green Road
Buckle maker
Removed to 8 Finsbury Street,
Moorefields. (No date given)

13 July 1799
8 Finsbury Street
Plate worker

15 March 1802
8 Finsbury Street, Moorefields
Plate worker

25 November 1803
8 Finsbury Street
Plate worker

⊕ 17 August 1805
8 Finsbury Street
Plate worker

 30 May 1810
8 Finsbury Street
Plate worker

 ⊕ 31 October 1812
8 Finsbury Street
Spoon maker

 ⊕ 16 June 1815
8 Finsbury Street
Spoon maker

 14 March 1818
with Henry John Lias
8 Finsbury Street
Spoon maker

 2 April 1818
with Henry John Lias
8 Finsbury Street
Spoon maker

 ⊕ 9 October 1819
with Henry Lias
8 Finsbury Street
Spoon maker

⊕ Mark entered in two sizes

203

* 7 August 1823
with Henry and Charles Lias
8 Finsbury Street
Plate workers

 ⊕ 3 March 1828
with Henry and Charles Lias
8 Finsbury Street
Plate workers

 * 24 September 1830
with Henry John and Charles Lias
8 Finsbury Street, St Lukes
Plate workers

 26 August 1835
with Henry John and Charles Lias
8 Finsbury Street, St Lukes
Plate workers

 ⊕ 19 May 1837
with Henry Lias
Manufactory and residence 8 and 9
Finsbury Street, St Lukes
Plate workers

 28 November 1839
with Henry Lias
(Address as before)

⊕ Mark entered in two sizes
204 * Mark entered in three sizes

⊕ 13 February 1843
with Henry Lias
(Address as before)

And a new Manufactory, 7 Salisbury
Court, Fleet Street

30 July 1845
with Henry Lias
(Address as before)

Trading under the Firm of John Lias & Son,
8 May 1848

It is possible that these are the marks of two John Lias's,
presumably father and son, who were Buckle maker and
Plate worker respectively. This possibility has been
considered since the signatures against the marks of the
Buckle maker appear to be by a different John Lias from
those against the Plate worker. If this is correct, all those
marks entered from 13 July 1799 onwards would be by
John Lias (No 2).

There is no record of either John Lias being apprenticed
through the Goldsmiths' Company or becoming a Freeman of the Company.

Both Henry John and Charles, who were the sons of John
Lias (No 2), joined their father in partnership although
only Henry John became a Freeman of the Goldsmiths'
Company.

He was apprenticed to Isaac Boorman (Goldsmith) on
1 February 1809 and obtained his freedom on 7 August
1816. He eventually became Prime Warden of the
Company in 1861 and died in 1877.

⊕ Mark entered in two sizes

2 October 1704
N.S.

Hemings Row,
near St Martins Lane

5 September 1720
O.S.

Hemings Row,
near St Martins Lane

He was not apprenticed through the Goldsmiths' Company nor was he a Freeman of the Company.

He obtained his freedom of the Broderers' Company by Redemption on 19 September 1704 yet traded as a goldsmith.

He may have retired or died in 1730 when his son John, entered his own mark from the same address. It is known that he was dead by July 1735 when John obtained his own freedom.

John Liger

9 December 1730
O.S.

At the Sign of the Pearl,
in Hemings Row,
St Martin's Lane

He was not apprenticed through the Goldsmiths' Company nor was he a Freeman of the Company.

He was the son of Isaac Liger who traded as a Goldsmith although he was a Freeman of the Broderers' Company.

Since John obtained his freedom of the Broderers' Company by Patrimony on 2 July 1735, he was evidently born after September 1704, this being the date of his father's freedom.

April 1697
Cripplegate Without

24 January 1698
without Cripplegate

He was the son of John Lock and was apprenticed to
Roger Strickland on 21 May 1680. He obtained his
freedom on 20 July 1687, was made a Liveryman in
1698 and an Assistant in 1709.
William Fleming was apprenticed to him in 1687.

30 March 1731
Maiden Lane, Wood Street

As the widow of Matthew Lofthouse (No 1), she carried
on the family business following her husband's death
in 1731.

Their son Matthew (No 2) obtained his freedom on 6
June 1732.

28 June 1705
N.S.
Temple Bar Without
Free Wax Chandler

26 January 1721
O.S.
Temple Bar Without

He was not a Freeman of the Goldsmiths' Company.

He was the son of Alvara Lofthouse (Yeoman) of Menston,
Yorkshire and was apprenticed to George Dawson (or
Hawson), a member of the Wax Chandlers' Company, on
20 February 1688—89. He obtained his freedom of that
Company on 29 September 1697 and was made a Livery-
man in October 1716.

In 1731 he died leaving his widow Mary, to carry on the
business.

His son Matthew (No 2) was apprenticed to John
Boddington, a member of the Goldsmiths' Company on
16 October 1724. He was turned over to Matthew (No 1)
on 17 October 1724 and obtained his freedom of the
Goldsmiths' Company on 6 June 1732.

Matthew (No 1)'s brother, Seth Lofthouse, also traded as
a Goldsmith but was a member of the Merchant Taylors'
Company.

April 1697
Bishopsgate Street

The above entry in the records states Seth Lofthouse was a
Wax Chandler but this appears to have been added at a
later date and to be an incorrect statement, since he was
a Freeman of the Merchant Taylors' Company.

He was the son of Alvara Lofthouse of Menston, Yorkshire
and was apprenticed to William Wakefield of St Nicholas
Lane on 16 February 1675. (Although Wakefield traded
as a Goldsmith, he was a member of the Merchant Taylors'
Company). Seth obtained his freedom of the Merchant
Taylors' Company on 25 September 1683 and was made
a Liveryman on 5 December 1701.

His son Joseph was apprenticed to Matthew Derousseau,
a member of the Goldsmiths' Company in 1705 but there
is no record of his obtaining his freedom of the Company.

William Bellassyse was apprenticed to Seth in 1709.

Seth's brother, Matthew Lofthouse (No 1), also traded as
a Goldsmith although be became a member of the Wax
Chandlers' Company.

31 July 1699
In Gutter Lane

10 June 1725
O.S.
In the Strand

He was the son of Samuel Lukin (Gentleman) of Bodicote,
Oxfordshire and was apprenticed to St John Hoyte
(Goldsmith) on 21 June 1692. At a later date he was
turned over to John Sheppard and obtained his freedom
of the Goldsmiths' Company on 5 July 1699.

He was made a Liveryman in October 1708 and resigned
from the Company on 15 October 1755.

2 December 1702
Ball Alley
Lombard Street

He was not apprenticed through the Goldsmiths' Company
nor was he a Freeman of the Company.

Probably his father was Matthew Madden.

Matthew Madden

April 1697
Ball Alley
Lombard Street

April 1697
Ball Alley
Lombard Street

He was not apprenticed through the Goldsmiths' Company
nor was he a Freeman of the Company.

Probably Jonathan Madden was his son.

20 January 1777
with Richard Carter
Bartholomew Close
Plate workers

He obtained his freedom of the Goldsmiths' Company by
Redemption on 4 April 1759, was made a Liveryman in
1763 and an Assistant in 1787.

He became 4th Warden in 1792, 3rd Warden in 1793,
2nd Warden in 1794 and Prime Warden in 1795.

It appears that he died between 1796 and 1801.

His two sons, Robert (No 2) and Thomas were apprenticed
to him in 1776 and 1778 respectively and both obtained
their freedoms in 1788.

⊕ 18 January 1794
with Thomas Makepeace
Serle Street, Lincoln's Inn Fields
Plate workers

⊕ 20 January 1795
Serle Street, Lincoln's Inn
Plate worker

He was the son of Robert Makepeace (No 1), Goldsmith of Serle Street and was apprenticed to his father on 7 February 1776.

He obtained his freedom of the Company on 2 April 1788, was made a Liveryman in 1791 and an Assistant in 1801.

He became 4th Warden in 1812, 3rd Warden in 1813 and then Prime Warden in 1814. He died in 1827.

His brother, Thomas, was apprenticed to Robert (No 1) on 7 October 1778 and obtained his freedom on 7 May 1788.

⊕ Mark entered in two sizes.

19 August 1706
St Martins Lane
Free of the Butchers' Company

September 1720
O.S.
St Martins Lane

He was never a Freeman of the Goldsmiths' Company.

He was the son of Samuel Margas and was apprenticed to
Thomas Jenkins, a member of the Butchers' Company,
on 2 January 1698—99. He obtained his freedom of that
Company on 7 August 1706.

His son Samuel, was apprenticed to him and later practised
as a silversmith.

14 February 1714—15
N.S.
King Street,
Covent Garden

8 March 1720—21
O.S.
King Street,
Covent Garden

He was never a Freeman of the Goldsmiths' Company.

He was the son of Anne and Jacob Margas and was
apprenticed to his father on 8 January 1707—8.

Although his father was a Freeman of the Butchers'
Company, he traded as a goldsmith.

Samuel became a member of the Butchers' Company when
he obtained his freedom on 12 January 1714—15.

His son, Samuel, obtained his freedom of the Butchers'
Company by Patrimony on 6 August 1745.

24 April 1744
St Swithin's Lane,
Lombard Street
Removed to Lombard Street, 4 August 1749
Removed to Cornhill, 6 February 1761

He was the son of George Marsh and was apprenticed to
William Lukin on 30 September 1726 but was turned over
to Gabriel Sleath on 2 November 1731.

He obtained his freedom on 6 November 1741.

John Matthew

13 September 1710
Ball Alley,
Lombard Street

He was the son of Mary and William Matthew (No 1) and
was apprenticed to his father on 6 July 1704.

Due to his father's death, he probably did not complete
his apprenticeship by service, since he obtained his
freedom by Patrimony on 6 September 1710.

His brother was William Matthew (No 2).

Widow of William Matthew

28 May 1707

George Alley,
Lombard Street

She was the wife of William Matthew (No 1). She took over the family business when her husband died in 1707.

Two of her sons, William (No 2) and John became Freemen of the Goldsmiths' Company.

V **William Matthew (No 1)**

April 1697

Foster Lane

20 April 1700

George Alley,
Lombard Street

He was the son of Thomas Matthew and was apprenticed to John Smith on 28 July 1675. He obtained his freedom on 27 June 1683.

When he died in 1707, his wife Mary took over the business and entered her own mark.

He had two sons, William (No 2) and John, both of whom became Freemen of the Goldsmiths' Company.

17 March 1710—11
N.S.
In the Minories

 20 June 1720
O.S.
In the Minories

 1728
Bartlet Court in Bartlet Street,
Clerkenwell

He was the son of Mary and William Matthew (No 1) and was apprenticed to his father on 4 June 1701.

His father, having died in 1707, he obtained his freedom by Patrimony on 8 February 1711.

His brother was John Matthew.

18 December 1700
N.S.
In Pall Mall

26 August 1720
O.S.
In Pall Mall

He was the son of Samuel Mettayer and was apprenticed to David Willaume (No 1) on 29 September 1693.

He obtained his freedom on 17 December 1700 and was made a Liveryman in October 1712.

Both he and David Willaume were Huguenots. Marie Mettayer who was probably Louis' sister, was married to David Willaume (No 1) in 1690.

Louis' daughter, Susanna, obtained her freedom by Patrimony on 5 December 1738.

Louis' son, Samuel, obtained his freedom by Patrimony on 3 December 1741.

Circa
1746

This mark is not recorded at
Goldsmiths' Hall. Thought to be
Dorothy Mills & Thomas Sarbitt
and possibly entered in the
missing volume of Small Workers
marks.

6 April 1752
Saffron Hill

Probably she was the wife of Hugh Mills.

Following his death, she entered into partnership with
Thomas Sarbitt in about 1746.

Although she entered a mark in her own name in April
1752, by December 1753 she appears to have married
Thomas Sarbitt and entered another mark under the
name of Dorothy Sarbitt.

(See under Sarbitt).

Hugh Mills

23 May 1739
At the Sieve on Saffron Hill

14 February 1745—46
Blew Court, Saffron Hill

He was not apprenticed through the Goldsmiths' Company
nor was he a Freeman of the Company.

Dorothy Mills, who appears to have been his wife, entered
into partnership with Thomas Sarbitt following his
death about 1746.

April 1697
Bridewell precinct

He was the son of Samuel Moore and obtained his freedom by Patrimony on 15 July 1664.

Thomas Morse

   N.S.

5 September 1720
At the Spotted Dog
in Lombard Street.

   O.S.

He was the son of Thomas Morse and was apprenticed to Isaac Maylin (Goldsmith) on 7 March 1710. At a later date he was turned over to Anthony Nelme and obtained his freedom of the Goldsmiths' Company on 7 April 1720.

Prior
to
1697

Only recorded at Goldsmiths' Hall in 1722 under Francis, his son. Where found on silverware prior to 1697, it is presumed to be an Antony Nelme mark which was entered in the now missing records.

April 1697
Ave Maria Lane

April 1697
Ave Maria Lane

He was the son of John Nelme and was apprenticed to Richard Rowley on 1 November 1672. At a later date he was turned over to Isaac Deighton, presumably due to the death of Richard Rowley. He obtained his freedom on 16 January 1679 and was made an Assistant in 1703. He was made 4th Warden in 1717, 2nd Warden in 1722 but died the same year leaving his son, Francis, to carry on the business.

His son, Francis, was apprenticed to him in 1711 and obtained his freedom in 1719. Another son called Younger was apprenticed to Roger Hudson in 1713 but there is no record of his obtaining his freedom. Another son, John, was apprenticed to Antony in 1718 and obtained his freedom by Patrimony in 1725.

20 March 1722—23
Ave Maria Lane
The same marks as
Antony Nelme

19 June 1739
Ave Maria Lane

He was the son of Antony Nelme and was apprenticed to
his father on 6 March 1711. He obtained his freedom on
9 April 1719 and was made a Liveryman in October 1721.

When his father died in 1722, Francis carried on the
family business using the same marks as his father.

224

6 June 1798
Berkeley Street, Clerkenwell
Plate worker

3 December 1799
Berkeley Street, Clerkenwell
Removed to 9 Cross Street,
Hatton Garden,
4 March 1800

Presumably she was the wife of Thomas Northcote and
took over the family business when Thomas died in
1798.

20 August 1776
Shoemakers Row, Blackfriars
Spoon maker

29 October 1777
Shoemakers Row, Blackfriars

27 April 1779
Shoemakers Row, Blackfriars

Removed to Berkeley Street,
St Johns Gate, 13 January 1781

16 May 1782
Berkeley Street
Spoon maker

19 November 1784
13 Berkeley Street, Clerkenwell
Plate worker

27 November 1784
13 Berkeley Street, Clerkenwell
Plate worker

4 December 1786
13 Berkeley Street, Clerkenwell
Plate worker

5 March 1789
Berkeley Street
Spoon maker

19 August 1789
13 Berkeley Street, Clerkenwell
Plate worker

10 July 1792
13 Berkeley Street, Clerkenwell
Plate worker

5 June 1794
with George Bourne
Berkeley Street, Clerkenwell
Plate workers

11 July 1797
Berkeley Street, Clerkenwell

He was the son of Richard Northcote, was apprenticed to
Charles Hutton on 11 January 1764 and turned over to
Thomas Chawner on 23 June 1766. He obtained his
freedom on 3 July 1771, was made a Liveryman in
March 1781 and died in 1798 when Hannah, who was
presumably his wife, entered her own mark.

9 April 1796
38 Noble Street, Foster Lane
Plate worker

17 June 1808
with Robert Hennell (No 2)
38 Noble Street, Foster Lane
Plate workers

3 October 1809
38 Noble Street, Foster Lane
Plate worker

He was the son of William Nutting and was apprenticed to
Charles Wright on 3 July 1782. On 4 February 1784, he
was turned over to Thomas Chawner and obtained his
freedom on 6 January 1790.

His son, Henry, was apprenticed to him in 1808 and
obtained his freedom in 1816.

Joseph Angel (No 2) was apprenticed to Henry, senior
in 1796.

3 July 1739
Houndsditch

He was not apprenticed through the Goldsmiths' Company nor was he a Freeman of the Company.

Charles Overing

April 1697
Carey Lane

He was the son of Thomas Overing and was apprenticed to John Cruttall on 13 October 1680. He obtained his freedom on 8 June 1692.

His son, Thomas, obtained his freedom by Patrimony on 21 February 1716. His other son, John, was apprenticed to John East on 7 September 1715 but was turned over to Charles Overing on 22 February 1716 and obtained his freedom by Patrimony on 5 October 1721. Also related to Charles was James Overing. Possibly they were brothers.

Richard Bayley was apprenticed to Charles Overing and John Gibbons in 1699.

7 October 1717
Carey Lane

He was not apprenticed through the Goldsmiths' Company nor was he a Freeman of the Company.

He was possibly a brother of Charles Overing.

His son, also a James, was apprenticed to Edward Holaday on 31 May 1717 and later turned over to Charles Overing presumably due to Edward Holaday's death.

There is no record of James junior having obtained his freedom.

April 1698
Hemings Row,
near St Martins Lane

He was the son of Daniel Paillet and was apprenticed to
Thomas Symonds on 1 August 1688. He obtained his
freedom on 10 January 1695.

Lewis Pantin (No 1)

21 March 1733–34
Castle Street, near Leicester Fields

29 June 1739
Leicester Fields

He was the son of Mary and Simon Pantin (No 2) and took
over the family business from his mother in 1734.
He never became a Freeman of the Goldsmiths' Company.
Lewis Pantin (No 2) was probably his son.

28 July 1768
45 Fleet Street

19 October 1782
36 Southampton Street,
Strand
Goldworker

22 March 1788
36 Southampton Street,
Strand
Goldworker

12 April 1792
8 Sloane Square, Chelsea
Goldworker

Removed to 6 Crown Street,
Westminster, 30 October 1795

Removed to 17 Alfred Place,
Newington Causeway, 10 July 1800

He was probably the son of Lewis Pantin (No 1) and obtained his freedom by Redemption on 11 March 1767 presumably because his father was not a member of the Goldsmiths' Company.

He was made a Liveryman in November 1776 and died between 1802 and 1811. His son was Lewis Pantin (No 3).

20 December 1798
62 St Martins-le-Grand
Small worker

22 June 1802
30 Marsham Street, Westminster
Goldworker

Removed to 5 Canterbury,
New Manor Place, Walworth, 17 July 1805

He was the son of Lewis Pantin (No 2) and obtained his
freedom by Patrimony on 3 July 1799.

Mary Pantin   P

14 August 1733
Green Street, Leicester Fields

She was the wife of Simon Pantin (No 2). When her
husband died in 1733, she took over the family business.
Early in 1734 she handed over the business to her son
Lewis Pantin (No 1).

23 June 1701
St Martins Lane

16 September 1717
In Castle Street

30 June 1720
O.S.
In Castle Street

He was apprenticed to Pierre Harache (No 1) and obtained his freedom on 4 June 1701. He was made a Liveryman in October 1712 and probably died early in 1729 when his son Simon (No 2) took over the business.

Simon (No 2) was apprenticed to him in 1717.

Augustin Courtauld was apprenticed to him in 1701 and Peter Courtauld in 1705.

4 February 1728—9
Castle Street, near Leicester Field,
St Martin in the Fields

23 February 1730—1
Green Street, Leicester Field

He was the son of Simon Pantin (No 1) and was apprenticed
to his father on 23 May 1717. There is no record of his
obtaining his freedom but this was not necessary as his
business address was outside the city precincts. When he
died in 1733, his wife Mary took over the business.

Their son was Lewis Pantin (No 1).

Sarah Parr

20 June 1728
Cheapside

She was the wife of Thomas Parr (No 1) and upon his
death in 1728 continued running the family business.

Their son, Thomas (No 2), appears to have taken over the
firm when he entered his own mark in 1733.

Their daughter, Elizabeth, obtained her freedom of the
Goldsmiths' Company by Patrimony on 27 July 1738 but
does not appear to have entered a mark of her own.

April 1697
Wood Street

 19 August 1717
Cheapside

He was the son of Henry Parr (Clerk) of Cork, Ireland, and was apprenticed to Simon Noy (Goldsmith) on 9 September 1687. He obtained his freedom on 8 August 1694 and was made a Liveryman in October 1712.

Upon his death in 1728, his wife Sarah continued running the business, entering her own mark in June of that year. His son was Thomas Parr (No 2).

Humphrey Payne was turned over as an apprentice to Thomas Parr (No 1) on 15 July 1694. Presumably this was permitted by the Goldsmiths' Company knowing that Parr would formally become a Freeman of the Company on the 8 August following.

9 February 1732—33
Cheapside
Goldsmith

19 June 1739
Cheapside
Goldsmith

He was the son of Thomas Parr (No 1) and obtained his
freedom of the Goldsmiths' Company by Patrimony on
5 March 1733.

He was made a Liveryman in January 1750 and an
Assistant in 1753.

He became 4th Warden in 1771, 3rd Warden in 1772 and
2nd Warden in 1773.

3 December 1701
N.S.
Gutter Lane

3 December 1701
N.S.
Gutter Lane

1720
O.S.
Cheapside
(At the sign of the Hen and Chickens)

15 June 1739
Cheapside
Goldsmith

He was the son of Nicholas Payne and was apprenticed
to Roger Grainge on 15 August 1694. At a later date he
was turned over to Thomas Parr (No 1). He obtained his
freedom on 21 November 1701.

In 1708 he became a Liveryman and in 1734 an Assistant
of the Goldsmiths' Company. He was made 4th Warden in
1747, 3rd Warden in 1748, and 2nd Warden in 1749. Early
in 1751, he handed his business over to his son, John, and
retired to Daventry, Northamptonshire where he died on
1 August 1751.

Robert Cox was apprenticed to him in 1744. Humphrey's
son, John was apprenticed to him in 1732.

13 April 1751
Cheapside

Circa
1761

In the Goldsmiths' Company's own
silver collection this mark is to be
found on two items of plate which
are known to have been
commissioned from John Payne.
Possibly the mark was entered
in one of the missing volumes
of marks.

He was the son of Humphrey Payne and was apprenticed
to his father on 11 January 1732—3. He obtained his
freedom on 7 February 1739—40, was made a Liveryman
in 1740 and an Assistant in 1747.

He became 4th Warden in 1760, 3rd Warden in 1761,
2nd Warden in 1762 and Prime Warden in 1765.

In 1751 he took over the family business, following his
father's retirement, and entered his own mark in April
of that year.

1 February 1703—4
In the Strand,
near the New Exchange

28 July 1720
O.S.
In the Strand,
near the New Exchange

He was the son of Edmond Pearce, of Tewkesbury and
was apprenticed to Henry Beesley on 11 August 1693.
At a later date he was turned over to Philip Rolles,
presumably due to Henry Beesley's death.

Edmond obtained his freedom on 24 January 1704.

8 January 1745—46
In New Rents, St Martins-le-Grand
Removed to Deans Court
8 August 1749

12 July 1756
with Robert Peaston
St Martins-le-Grand

Neither William or Robert Peaston were apprenticed through the Goldsmiths' Company nor were they Freemen of the Company.

Although they worked within the city boundaries, they would be exempt from becoming Freemen as their address of St Martins-le-Grand was situated in a "Liberty" area.

They may have been brothers although it is more probable that Robert was William's son. Records show that Robert was dead by 5 August 1778, the date when his son, William, the Younger, was apprenticed to yet another William Peaston of Jewins Street who had become a Free Goldsmith in 1768.

1 May 1741
Orange Street
near Leicester Fields

She presumably was the wife of John Pero and took over
the business from him in 1741 probably because of his
death.

She re-entered John's last mark as her own but with the
lower portion removed.

24 August 1717
in the Strand

23 November 1732
Suffolk Street

22 June 1739
Orange Street
Free Goldsmith

He was the son of John Pero and was apprenticed to
Thomas Farren on 30 June 1709. He obtained his freedom
on 12 July 1717 and was made a Liveryman in March
1739. He probably died in 1741 when Isabel Pero, who
was presumably his wife, took over the business and re-
entered his last mark as her own but with the lower part
removed.

His son, Edward, was apprenticed to Charles Gardner
in 1740 but there is no record of his obtaining his
freedom.

Jean Petry

21 November 1707
In the Pall Mall

He was the son of Bartholomew Petry and was apprenticed
to David Willaume (No 1) on 25 July 1700. He obtained
his freedom on 21 November 1707.

Thomas Phipps

8 July 1783
with Edward Robinson
40 Gutter Lane
Small workers

8 August 1789
with Edward Robinson
40 Gutter Lane

With Edward Robinson and
James Phipps

(No date or address. Presumably
entered between 22 June 1811 and
4 July 1811 being the dates of
the previous and following entries)

31 January 1816
with James Phipps
Gutter Lane, Cheapside

He was the son of James Phipps and was apprenticed to
his father to learn the trade of goldsmith on 5 April
1769. He obtained his freedom on 7 May 1777, was made
a Liveryman in February 1791 and died on 31 October
1823.

His son, James, was apprenticed to him on 5 February
1800 and obtained his freedom on 1 April 1807.

Another son, John, obtained his freedom by Patrimony
in 1801 but appears to have become an attorney.

Daniel Piers

3 November 1746
Spur Street

He was not apprenticed through the Goldsmiths' Company
nor was he a Freeman of the Company.

He appears to have died in 1758 when his wife, Mary,
took over the family business.

Mary Piers

4 June 1758
Spur Street, Leicester Fields

She was the wife of Daniel Piers. When he
died in 1758, she took over the family business.

(No date given)
N.S.
Chandos Street

(No date given)
O.S.
Chandos Street
Free Goldsmith

(Presumably these
two marks were
entered between
2 July 1724 and
August 1724.)

29 June 1739
Chandos Street
Goldsmith

His parents, Alexis Pilleau and Madeleine Pezé had been
married in 1683. Father was a merchant goldsmith of
Le Mans, France.

In 1688 they had come to England as Huguenot refugees
and by 1697 father was plying his trade of goldsmith and
maker of artificial teeth in St Martins Lane.

They had four sons and one daughter; Jean who remained
in France and became a master goldsmith, Alexis Pierre
born March 1692 and died July 1692, Alexis Pezé who
became a goldsmith, René who died young between
April 1727 and September 1730 and daughter Madeleine
Louise born December 1693 and dead by 1730.

Alexis Pezé was born on 13 January 1696 and was apprenticed to Jean Chartier on 27 April 1710 when fourteen years old. He obtained his freedom of the Goldsmiths' Company on 2 July 1724 and subsequently entered his first mark in the records at some date prior to August 1724, this being the entry date of a following maker's mark.

On 25 December 1724 he married Henrietta Chartier, who is thought to have been his master's daughter. They had six sons and two daughters. In the autumn of 1730, his father died leaving him the business.

Alexis Pezé eventually died circa 1762-63, by which time his wife, together with five of his sons and one daughter were already dead.

Although Alexis Pezé is generally known as 'Pezé junior' or Pezé son of Pezé as entered in the records at Goldsmiths Hall, this is not strictly correct. It seems that he dropped his first baptismal name of Alexis and used only Pezé which had been his mother's maiden name. Likewise, although his father's real name was Alexis, records at Goldsmiths Hall describe him in one entry as Pezé father of Peze who was apprenticed to Jean Chartier on 27 April 1710 and in another entry as Alexander Pillio, goldsmith of St Martin in the Fields and father of René who was apprenticed to John Penkethman on 6 August 1712.

25 November 1737
At Black Moor's Head,
at the corner of York Buildings
in the Strand

He was not apprenticed through the Goldsmiths' Company
nor was he a Freeman of the Company.

He was probably related to Pierre Platel, the goldsmith,
possibly being the son of Pierre's brother, Claude
Platel.

28 June 1699
Pall Mall

He was the son of Sieur Jean Batiste Bertrand Platel du Plateau, Esquire of Ecrose St Dizier. In 1685, Pierre with his father and brother Claude, fled to Flanders from the religious persecutions in France. In 1688 they came to England where on 8 May 1697 he and brother Claude took out letters of denization.

Being a Huguenot, Pierre obtained his freedom by Redemption on 14 June 1699 by order of the Court of Aldermen. He was made a Liveryman in October 1708 and died on 21 May 1719.

Philip Rainaud was apprenticed to him in 1700.

Paul de Lamerie was apprenticed to him in 1703.

Pierre had a son, Pierre, born 19 September 1701 and a daughter, Martha, born on 8 February 1703. Pierre junior became a vicar in 1732 and died in 1769.

8 April 1755
Foster Lane
Removed into Gutter Lane,
11 September 1757

17 March 1774
47 Gutter Lane
Plate worker

7 May 1789
47 Gutter Lane
Plate worker

He never became a Freeman of the Goldsmiths' Company.

He was the son of George Plummer (Grasior) of Evington,
Leicestershire and was apprenticed, for the fee of £21, to
Edward Aldridge, a member of the Clothworkers' Company
who traded as a Goldsmith, on 4 February 1746.

This Edward Aldridge was the one who traded from
Foster Lane and was not the Edward Aldridge junior of
Green Street, Leicester Fields, who was also a Goldsmith.

William Plummer obtained his freedom of the Clothworkers'
Company on 5 February 1755.

His son, William, was apprenticed to Thomas
Whipham junior (Goldsmith) on 5 November but
there is no record of his obtaining his freedom.

16 October 1734
Over against the Bird in Hand,
in Long Acre

26 June 1739
Long Acre
Removed to Belton Street,
Long Acre
26 January 1743–4

He was not apprenticed through the Goldsmiths'
Company, nor was he a Freeman of the Company.

12 October 1749
with William Shaw (No 2)
Maiden Lane
Removed to Wood Street
2 January 1750

27 June 1759
with William Shaw (No 2)

Circa 1766

This mark is not recorded at Goldsmiths' Hall. Possibly William & James Priest

He was the son of William Priest and was apprenticed to Richard Gurney on 30 July 1740. He obtained his freedom on 6 September 1749, was made a Liveryman in March 1758 and died between 1802 and 1811.
His brother, James, was apprenticed to him on 7 December 1750 and obtained his freedom on 4 July 1764.

April 1697
St Martins-le-Grand

April 1697
St Martins-le-Grand

He was the son of Humfrey Pyne, was apprenticed to George Bowers on 23 October 1667 and obtained his freedom on 1 September 1676. He was made an Assistant of the Company in 1703, 4th Warden in 1715, 3rd Warden in 1720, 2nd Warden in 1721 and Prime Warden in 1725.

In 1727, following his bankruptcy, he applied for and obtained the lowly position of Beadle of the Goldsmiths' Company provided he resigned from all official positions in the company. He died in 1732 still in debt and soon after, his daughters Mary and Ann petitioned the Company for a pension as they were destitute. They received £5 per annum for life. On 7 February 1737 they both obtained their freedom of the Goldsmiths' Company by Patrimony.

His son, Benjamin, was apprenticed to him on 21 October 1708 and obtained his freedom on 18 May 1716. He became Assistant Assayer of the Company in 1720 and died in 1737.

(No date. After 3 July 1739 being the date of entry of a previous maker's mark)

Huggin Alley, Wood Street

30 May 1754

He was the son of Thomas Quantock and was apprenticed to James Gould on 14 January 1725–6. He obtained his freedom on 9 January 1738–9.

A John Quantock was entered in the Parliamentary Return of 1773 as a plate worker in Wood Street. Presumably this was the same person or else his son.

14 February 1706—7
At corner of Suffolk Street

26 October 1720
O.S.
At corner of Suffolk Street

He was the son of James Rainaud of Rcthsoire in Pitou
Province, France and was apprenticed to Pierre Platel
on 29 May 1700. He obtained his freedom on 13
February 1706—7 and was made a Liveryman in October
1721.

He appears to have become bankrupt in 1728.

April 1697
St Martins-le-Grand

April 1697
St Martins-le-Grand

He obtained his freedom by Redemption on 11 August
1697 by order of the Court of Aldermen. He was made a
Liveryman in October 1698.

3 July 1817
12 Well Street
Plate worker

28 October 1819
9 Brook Street, Holborn
Small worker

13 June 1822
12 Well Street
Plate worker

12 October 1826
12 Well Street
Plate worker

24 October 1826
12 Well Street
Plate worker

* 6 April 1829
with William Summers
Brook Street, Holborn
Small workers
Removed to 10 Great Marlborough
Street, Regent Street,
9 January 1839

* Mark entered in three sizes

258

* 2 December 1840
with William Summers
(No address. Presumably at
10 Great Marlborough Street)

Apparently he had two separate premises at the same time,
one at Brook Street for small works and the other at Well
Street for plate work.

It seems unlikely that there could have been two Charles
Rawlings, one working from each address, since the
signature against each of the above marks in the Companys'
records appears to be by the same Charles Rawlings.

He does not appear to have been apprenticed through the
Goldsmiths' Company and he did not become a Freeman
of the Company although a Charles Rawlings, son of
William Rawlings (Capillaire maker), was apprenticed to
Richard Coleman on 7 March 1810 but only to learn the
trade of a watch finisher.

There is no record of this Charles obtaining his freedom
of the Goldsmiths' Company.

N.B.   Capillaire was a syrup or infusion of maiden hair
fern. It is known that Ben Johnson used to add
it to his port wine.

* Mark entered in three sizes   259

17 October 1701
with Daniel Sleamaker
Laurence Pountney Lane

22 July 1704
Laurence Pountney Lane

He was the son of John Read and having been
apprenticed to John Archbold on 13 October 1686, he
was turned over to Robert Timbrell at a later date. He
obtained his freedom on 9 May 1694 and was made
a Liveryman in October 1708.

His partner, Daniel Sleamaker, was also apprenticed
to Robert Timbrell in 1690.

⊕ 10 October 1815
with David Reid

Dean Street, Newcastle

Plate workers

⊕ 30 July 1817

Dean Street, Newcastle

By virtue of a Power of Attorney
I enter four marks, (actually five),
of Christian Ker Reid of
Newcastle-upon-Tyne this ninth
day of July 1817.
(Signed) William Ker Reid,
Attorney to said Christian Ker Reid.

16 May 1828
with David Reid

Dean Street, Newcastle

(Entered) By virtue of above

(Signed)   William Ker Reid
           David Reid

N.B.   These marks are to be found likewise in the
       records of the Goldsmiths' Company of Newcastle-
       upon-Tyne where they are imprinted upon a
       copper plate.

⊕   Mark entered in two sizes

*   Mark entered in three sizes

He was a silversmith in Newcastle-upon-Tyne from 1778 until his death on 18 September 1834.

Apparently, he moved to Newcastle from Edinburgh to work for the silversmith, John Langlands with a view to an eventual partnership.

However, Langlands took John Robertson into partnership instead, so Reid set up in business on his own and founded the present-day firm of Reid & Sons.

His two sons, William Ker and David, became silversmiths; William moved to London where he became a Freeman of the Goldsmiths' Company in 1814 while David remained in Newcastle and joined his father in partnership. Neither Christian nor David ever became Freemen of the London or Newcastle Companies of Goldsmiths. After Christian's death in 1834, his son David continued to run the family business in Newcastle.

Both William Ker and David married daughters of the goldsmith Edward Barnard (No 1).

William Ker and Mary married on 11 February 1812 and had thirteen children while David and Elizabeth married on 26 August 1815 and produced ten children.

N.B.   These marks are to be found likewise in the records of the Goldsmiths' Company of Newcastle-upon-Tyne where they are imprinted upon a copper plate.

8 June 1812
with Joseph Craddock
67 Leather Lane
Plate workers

19 August 1819
with Joseph Craddock
3 Carey Street, Lincoln Inn Fields

24 September 1824
with Joseph Craddock
3 Carey Street, Lincoln Inn Fields

8 November 1825
5 Bream's Building, Chancery Lane
Plate worker

21 February 1826
5 Bream's Building, Chancery Lane

3 May 1828
5 Bream's Building, Chancery Lane

His father, who was Christian Ker Reid, a silversmith of Newcastle-upon-Tyne from 1778 until his death in 1834, was founder of the present day Newcastle firm of Reid & Sons.

William's brother David and later his nephew Christian John continued to run the Newcastle firm after the death of Christian Ker Reid.

At some time William Ker Reid came to London where, in 1812, he became a partner with Joseph Craddock. On 2 November 1814, William obtained his freedom by Redemption of the Goldsmiths' Company in London. He was made a Liveryman in April 1818 and died on 1 February 1868.

His son, Edward Ker Reid, was apprenticed to him in 1836 but obtained his freedom by Patrimony in 1842. He was made a Liveryman in 1848 and died in 1886.

Another son, William Ker, was apprenticed to Edward Ker in 1846 but did not become a Freeman of the Goldsmiths' Company. He died in 1855 when 23 years old.

It is interesting to note that in October 1815, July 1817 and May 1828, the Newcastle partnership marks of Christian Ker Reid and David Reid (William's father and brother) were entered in the London records "by virtue of a power of Attorney" signed by William Ker Reid.

⊕ 1 January 1829
with George Storer

6 Carey Lane

Plate workers

Removed to 3 Lovell's Court,
Paternoster Row, 26 June 1835

Removed to 6 Carey Lane
16 February 1836

⊕ 18 June 1840
with George Storer

(No address. Presumably at
6 Carey Lane)

He was not apprenticed through the Goldsmiths' Company
nor was he a Freeman of the Company.

He was probably the son of John Reily of 6 Carey Lane
and carried on the family business when John retired or
died.

⊕ Mark entered in two sizes.

⊕ 28 November 1799
with Mary Hyde
6 Carey Lane
Small workers

20 February 1801
6 Carey Lane
Small worker

24 September 1802
6 Carey Lane

⊕ 15 February 1805
6 Carey Lane

9 April 1823
6 Carey Lane

13 June 1823
6 Carey Lane

He was not apprenticed through the Goldsmiths' Company
nor was he a Freeman of the Company.

Charles Reily was probably his son.

⊕ Mark entered in two sizes.

19 July 1818
12 Middle Row, Holborn
Plate worker

He was not apprenticed through the Goldsmiths' Company
nor was he a Freeman of the Company.

16 July 1724
N.S.
In St Martins Lane

O.S. (No date of entry given.
         Presumably it was 16 July 1724
         as above)
In St Martins Lane

He was the son of Stephen Ribouleau and was apprenticed
to Augustin Courtauld (No 1) on 5 July 1716. He
obtained his freedom on 2 July 1724.

13 June 1765
At the back of Tottenham Court Road,
near Whitfield Chapel in the Row

15 August 1780
14 Tottenham Court Road
Buckle maker

He was not apprenticed through the Goldsmiths' Company
nor was he a Freeman of the Company.

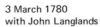

3 March 1780
with John Langlands

Plate workers at
Newcastle-upon-Tyne

(These marks were entered at the
Goldsmiths' Hall "by virtue of a
Letter of Attorney")

He never became a Freeman of the Goldsmiths' Company
of Newcastle-upon-Tyne.

In 1778 he became a partner with John Langlands, a
Newcastle silversmith. When Langlands died in 1793, his
wife continued the partnership with Robertson until its
dissolution on 10 June 1795 when Robertson entered
into partnership with David Darling.

In 1798, Robertson commenced working on his own. This
continued until about 1801.

One Ann Robertson, who may have been his wife, traded
from about 1801 to 1808.

His son, John Robertson (No 2), was apprenticed to
Thomas Watson on 11 March 1799 and in about 1811
went into partnership with John Walton.

20 October 1774
5 St John Street
Plate worker
(At) 67 Aldersgate Street,
18 July 1781

7 August 1787
(No address given)
Removed to 13 Clerkenwell Green,
5 February 1794

He was the son of John Robins of Bruton, Somerset and was apprenticed to Richard Wade on 3 October 1764. On 27 January 1766 he was turned over to David Whyte.

He obtained his freedom on 6 November 1771.

Thomas Robins, a relative, was apprenticed to him on 6 December 1786.

⊕ 10 June 1801
35 St Johns Square
Plate worker

He was the son of Thomas Robins (Mason) of Bruton,
Somerset and was apprenticed to John Robins (Goldsmith) of Aldersgate Street, London on 6 December
1786. John was evidently a relative as his father also
resided in Bruton.

Thomas obtained his freedom of the Goldsmiths' Company
on 6 August 1794.

He was made a Liveryman in June 1811 and died on
22 August 1859.

⊕ Mark entered in two sizes.

8 July 1783
with Thomas Phipps
40 Gutter Lane
Small workers

8 August 1789
with Thomas Phipps
40 Gutter Lane

With Thomas & James Phipps
(No date or address. Presumably
entered between 22 June 1811 and
4 July 1811, being the dates of the
previous and following entries of
other makers)

He was the son of Edward Robinson and was apprenticed
to James Phipps, the father of Thomas Phipps, to learn
the trade of goldsmith on 7 October 1772. He obtained
his freedom on 2 February 1780, was made a Liveryman
in February 1791 and died on 10 January 1816.

11 October 1776
96 Bishopsgate Without
Plate worker

It is probable that she was the wife of Philip Roker (No 3)
in which case she presumably entered her mark in October
1776 when Philip retired or died.

13 September 1743
Bishopsgate Street
Goldsmith

He was the son of Philip Roker (No 2) and was apprenticed
to his father on 25 May 1737. He obtained his freedom by
Patrimony on 19 December 1743.
His brothers were Philip (No 3) and Matthew. Philip (No 3)
was apprenticed to him in 1744.

29 April 1755
Greenwich, Kent

He was the son of Philip Roker (No 2) and obtained his freedom by Patrimony on 12 June 1754.

He was entered in the Parliamentary Return of 1773 as a Spoon maker at Greenwich.

Philip Ludford Roker (No 1)

April 1697
Sherborne Lane

He was the son of Thomas Roker and was apprenticed to Edward Gladwyn on 26 April 1676. There is no record of his obtaining his freedom.

His son was Philip Roker (No 2).

James Fraillon was apprenticed to Philip (No 1) in 1699.

7 April 1720
N.S.
Long Acre

17 August 1720
O.S.
Long Acre

20 June 1739
King Street, Westminster
Goldsmith

Later removed to Greenwich

He was the son of Philip Roker (No 1) and was apprenticed to Joseph Barbutt on 1 November 1707. He obtained his freedom on 7 April 1720.

His sons were John, Philip (No 3) and Matthew.

28 June 1776
96 Bishopsgate Street Without
Spoon maker

He was the son of Philip Roker (No 2) and was apprenticed to his elder brother John on 10 January 1743—44. When he eventually obtained his freedom, it was by Patrimony on 1 December 1756.

Probably he continued working at his brother's premises in Bishopsgate Street and eventually took over the firm.

By the time of the Parliamentary Return of 1773 he was a Spoon maker of Bishopsgate Street so presumably an earlier mark to the one illustrated had been entered in one of the missing volumes of records.

It is probable that Elizabeth Roker was his wife in which case Philip presumably retired or died in October 1776 this being the date when she entered her own mark.

1697
Over against Bull Inn Court
in the Strand

He was the son of John Rollos and obtained his freedom of
the Goldsmiths' Company by Redemption on 11 August
1697. He was made a Liveryman of the Company in
October 1698.

His son was Philip Rollos (No 2).

Philip Rollos (No 2)

20 August 1705
In Heath Cock Court
in the Strand

28 September 1720
In Heath Cock Court
in the Strand

He was the son of Philip Rollos (No 1), Goldsmith at St
Martin-in-the-Fields, and was apprenticed to Dallington
Ayres (Goldsmith) on 2 December 1692. At a later date
he was turned over to his father and eventually obtained
his freedom on 26 July 1705. Probably the 'later date'
was when his father obtained his own freedom of the
Goldsmiths' Company. In October 1712, he was made a
Liveryman of the Company.

277

30 May 1754

Carolina Court, Saffron Hill

He was the son of Richard Rugg and was apprenticed to James Gould on 10 January 1737—38. He obtained his freedom on 3 September 1746.

His son, Richard Rugg (No 2) was apprenticed to him in 1763.

John Crouch was apprenticed to him in 1758.

18 March 1775
St John Square
Plate worker

The above mark may possibly be Richard Rugg (No 1) but
it is most likely to be Richard Rugg (No 2), since Richard
(No 1) was at least 50 years old at the time whereas Richard
(No 2) had obtained his freedom only five years previously.

He was the son of Richard Rugg (No 1) and was apprenticed
to his father on 2 November 1763. He obtained his freedom
on 7 November 1770, was made a Liveryman in December
1771 and died between 1795 and 1801.

He was listed in the Parliamentary Return of 1773 as a
Plate worker of St John Square, Clerkenwell, so
presumably an earlier mark to that of 1775 was entered
in one of the missing volumes of marks.

4 March 1819
16 Dean Street, Soho
Plate worker

25 May 1819
16 Dean Street, Soho

31 October 1822
16 Dean Street, Soho

He was the senior partner in the firm of Rundell, Bridge and Rundell.

Paul Storr ran the manufacturing side of the firm from 1807 until 1819. Other partners were John Bridge, Edmund Rundell and William Theed. Philip Rundell was very difficult to work with, being of violent disposition, sly, cunning and very suspicious. His employees nicknamed him "vinegar", while his calm natured partner John Bridge was called "oil". When Storr left in 1819, the firm had to enter a new mark at the Goldsmiths' Hall. This was Philip Rundell's. In 1823 he retired from the firm leaving John Bridge to take over.

11 October 1718
Little St Martins Lane,
near Long Acre

26 July 1722
Old Street,
at corner of Great Suffolk Street
Free Goldsmith

25 June 1739
Great Suffolk Street,
near the Haymarket
Free Goldsmith

He was the son of Hugh Le Sage and was apprenticed to
Louis Cuny on 7 May 1708. He obtained his freedom on
25 September 1718 and was made a Liveryman in April
1740.

His son, Simon, was apprenticed to him in 1742.

Edward Wakelin was apprenticed to him in 1730.

Richard Beale was turned over to John Hugh Le Sage in
1725 having previously been apprenticed to Jonathan
Newton in 1722.

5 April 1754
Great Suffolk Street,
Charing Cross

He was the son of John Hugh Le Sage and was apprenticed to his father and Peter Meure (Freeman of the Butchers' Company) on 6 May 1742. He obtained his freedom on 5 June 1755.

27 January 1755
with George Baskerville
New Inn Passage,
Clare Market

29 August 1755
Baldwin's Gardens

He was not apprenticed through the Goldsmiths' Company
nor was he a Freeman of the Company.

Dorothy Sarbitt   S

13 December 1753
Saffron Hill

She was not apprenticed through the Goldsmiths' Company
nor was she a Freeman of the Company.

She was formerly Dorothy Mills (see under Mills) and
apparently entered into partnership with Thomas Sarbitt
about 1746.

In April 1752 she entered her own mark as Dorothy Mills.

She appears to have become the wife of Thomas Sarbitt
at sometime and entered her own mark as Dorothy Sarbitt
in December 1753 possibly due to Thomas's death.

14 February 1826
54 Cornhill
Plate worker

.A·B·S.

13 October 1826
54 Cornhill

11 November 1826
54 Cornhill

11 November 1829
54 Cornhill

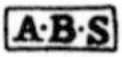

3 April 1830
54 Cornhill

26 January 1832
54 Cornhill

7 September 1833
with Joseph & Albert Savory
14 Cornhill

Plate workers and spoon makers

Factories at 15 Gee Street,
Goswell Street and at
5 Finsbury Place South

5 July 1834
with Joseph & Albert Savory
14 Cornhill

Factories at 15 Gee Street,
Goswell Street and at
5 Finsbury Place South

He was the son of Joseph Savory who had obtained his
freedom of the Goldsmiths' Company by Service on
3 February 1768. When Adey Bellamy obtained his
freedom by Patrimony on 6 October 1802 he was
trading as a Coal Merchant but by 1826, when he entered
his first mark, he was trading as a Goldsmith.

He had four sons: Thomas Cox, Albert, Joseph and Adey
Bellamy who became a bookseller. The other three
obtained their freedom by Patrimony; Thomas on
2 December 1829 and Albert and Joseph both on 4
December 1833.

T·C·S	13 September 1827 54 Cornhill Plate worker
T·C·S	2 November 1827 54 Cornhill
T·C·S	27 January 1832 54 Cornhill

He was the son of Adey Bellamy Savory (Goldsmith) and obtained his freedom by Patrimony on 2 December 1829 more than two years after he entered his first mark.

Presumably he worked with his father since both give their address as 54 Cornhill.

Thomas had three brothers; Adey Bellamy junior who became a bookseller, and Joseph and Albert who both obtained their freedom of the Goldsmiths' Company and joined their father in partnership.

24 September 1719
N.S.
Foster Lane
Free Broderer

24 June 1720
O.S.
Foster Lane

11 September 1723
O.S.

Although he traded as a silversmith, he was not apprenticed through the Goldsmiths' Company nor was he a Freeman of the Company.

He was the son of William Scarlett and was apprenticed to his father for seven years on 12 December 1710.

His father, who also traded as a silversmith, was a Freeman of the Broderers' Company which meant that when Richard obtained his own freedom by service on 5 February 1717, he likewise became a Freeman of the same Company.

April 1697
Foster Lane
Free Broderer

29 June 1720
O.S.
Foster Lane

25 September 1722
O.S.
Foster Lane

18 October 1725
O.S.
Foster Lane

He was the son of Thomas Scarlett and was apprenticed to
Simon Scott (Goldsmith) on 27 April 1687–8. Although
there is no record of his having obtained his freedom of the
Goldsmiths' Company, he did become a Freeman of the
Broderers' Company at some date prior to July 1694, this
being the date from when the Broderers' Company freedom
records have been preserved. At some later date, he became
a member of the Company's Court and eventually became its
Master in 1726.
His son Richard, who also became a silversmith by trade,
was apprenticed to him in 1710 and obtained his freedom
of the Broderers' Company in 1717.

10 February 1776
with Robert Jones
40 Bartholomew Close
Plate workers

13 January 1778
29 Bell Yard, Temple Bar
Plate worker

1 October 1787
29 Bell Yard

He was not apprenticed through the Goldsmiths' Company
nor was he a Freeman of the Company.

4 October 1802
with Benjamin Smith (No 1)
Lime Kiln Lane, Greenwich
Plate workers

21 March 1803
with Benjamin Smith (No 1)
Lime Kiln Lane, Greenwich

He was not apprenticed through the Goldsmiths' Company
nor was he a Freeman of the Company.

He worked in partnership with Benjamin Smith (No 1) for
the firm of Rundell, Bridge & Rundell at their Greenwich
workshops.

Circa
1763

(These marks are not recorded at
Goldsmiths' Hall.

Circa
1767 They are presumed to be Daniel
Smith and Robert Sharp and were
probably entered in the missing
volume of Large Workers marks.)

Circa
1769

9 December 1778
with Richard Carter
and Daniel Smith

14 Westmoreland Buildings

Plate workers

7 February 1780
with Daniel Smith

14 Westmoreland Buildings

(Note that two of the previous touch marks have been reused with the RC part removed. Presumably due to Richard Carter's death)

7 January 1788

14 Westmoreland Buildings, Aldersgate Street

Plate worker

(Note that the previous touch marks have been reused with the DS part removed)

He was the son of Robert Sharp (Yeoman of Newcastle-upon-Tyne) and, having been apprenticed to Gawen Nash (of the Goldsmiths' Company) on 4 February 1746, he was turned over on the same day to Thomas Gladwin (of the Merchant Taylors' Company).

He obtained his freedom of the Goldsmiths'
Company on 4 May 1757, was made a Liveryman
in December 1771 and died in 1803.

In the Parliamentry Return of 1773, he and his
partner Daniel Smith are recorded as plate workers of
Aldermanbury.

Another Robert Sharp, son of one John Sharp (Brewer
of Newcastle-upon-Tyne),was apprenticed to him in
1770 but there is no record of his having obtained
his freedom. Possibly he was a nephew of Robert.

Richard Sibley (No 1) was apprenticed to Daniel
Smith and Fendall Rushforth in 1785 and turned
over to Robert in 1791.

Daniel Smith's son, George, was apprenticed to him
in 1765 and obtained his freedom in 1772.

16 January 1727—8
O.S.
Gerrard Street, Soho

16 January 1727—8
N.S.
Gerrard Street, Soho

25 June 1739
Gerrard Street

24 April 1745
Gerrard Street

He was the son of Thomas Shaw (clerk) and was apprenticed to Edward Holliday on 9 March 1714. He obtained his freedom on 12 November 1724.

3 January 1748—9
Maiden Lane

12 October 1749
with William Priest
Maiden Lane
Removed to Wood Street
2 January 1750

27 June 1759
with William Priest

He was the son of Thomas Shaw (Dry Cooper) and was
apprenticed to John Swift on 11 November 1736. He
obtained his freedom on 6 April 1748 and was made a
Liveryman in April 1751.

In the Parliamentary Return of 1773, he is recorded as a
plate worker of Bishopsgate Street.

29 April 1700
Ball Alley
in Lombard Street

She was the wife of Joseph Sheene. When he died in 1700, she took over the family business.

Joseph Sheene

April 1697
Ball Alley
in Lombard Street

He was the son of Joseph Sheene and was apprenticed to Benjamin Bradford on 10 April 1677. For some reason his date of freedom does not appear to have been entered in the records and yet he was made a Liveryman in October 1698.

When he died in 1700, his widow, Alice, continued the family business.

14 November 1803
with Thomas Ellerton
14 Bartholomew Close
Plate workers

11 March 1805
14 Bartholomew Close
Plate worker

7 October 1805
with William Burwash
14 Bartholomew Close
Plate workers

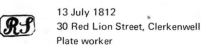

13 July 1812
30 Red Lion Street, Clerkenwell
Plate worker

He was the son of John Sibley and was apprenticed to
both Fendall Rushforth (Goldsmith) and Daniel Smith
(Merchant Taylor) on 2 November 1785. On 2 March
1791, he was turned over to Robert Sharp (Goldsmith).
He obtained his freedom on 2 October 1793, was made a
Liveryman in June 1811 and died in 1836. His sons
Richard (No 2) and Arthur were apprenticed to him in
1821 and 1831 respectively.

17 October 1701
with John Read
Laurence Pountney Lane

15 August 1704
St Swithins Lane

He was the son of Thomas Sleamaker and was apprenticed to Robert Timbrell on 14 January 1690–91. He obtained his freedom on 29 July 1698 and was made a Liveryman in April 1705.

His partner, John Read, was also apprenticed to Robert Timbrell in 1686.

14 March 1706–7
N.S.
Gutter Lane

17 June 1720
O.S.
Gutter Lane

18 June 1739
Gutter Lane

22 November 1753
with Francis Crump (No 1)
Gutter Lane

He was the son of Gabriel Sleath and was apprenticed to
Thomas Cooper on 27 November 1691. He obtained his
freedom on 22 October 1701 and was made a Liveryman
in October 1712.
Francis Crump (No 1) was apprenticed to him in 1726.
Francis Crump (No 2) was apprenticed to him in 1752.

4 October 1802
with Digby Scott
Lime Kiln Lane, Greenwich
Plate workers

21 March 1803
with Digby Scott
Lime Kiln Lane, Greenwich

11 May 1807
Lime Kiln Lane, Greenwich
Plate worker

25 June 1807
Lime Kiln Lane, Greenwich

23 February 1809
with James Smith
Lime Kiln Lane, Greenwich
Plate workers

14 October 1812
Lime Kiln Lane, Greenwich
Plate worker

Removed to Camberwell Terrace,
15 January 1814

5 July 1816
with Benjamin Smith (No 2)
Camberwell
Plate workers

25 June 1818
Camberwell
Plate worker

He was the son of Joseph Smith and was apprenticed to
Jonathan Bateman junior on 2 November 1791. He
obtained his freedom on 6 February 1799 (the same day
as William Bateman No 1) having completed his apprenticeship with the Bateman firm.

In 1802 he took up working with Digby Scott for the firm
of Rundell, Bridge & Rundell at their Greenwich factory.

Later, while still at the Greenwich factory, he worked with James Smith.

In 1814 he left Rundell's and moved to Camberwell where he continued doing work for Rundell's amongst his other commissions. In 1816 he entered a mark in partnership with his son Benjamin (No 2) who had been apprenticed to him in 1808.

Benjamin (No 1) died on 28 August 1823 after a long illness of over a year by which time his son had already taken over the business.

5 July 1816
with Benjamin Smith (No 1)
Camberwell
Plate workers

15 July 1818
Camberwell

24 May 1822
Removed to 12 Duke Street,
Lincoln Inn Fields

1 December 1837
12 Duke Street,
Lincoln Inn Fields

He was the son of Benjamin Smith (No 1) and was
apprenticed to his father on 6 July 1808. He obtained his
freedom on 3 January 1821, was made a Liveryman in
April 1842 and died in May 1850.

His son, Apsley, married Emma the daughter of G.R.
Elkington of Birmingham, who was famed for his
electro-plating process and manufacture of Elkington
Plateware.

303

Circa
1763

Circa
1767

These marks are not recorded
at Goldsmiths' Hall.

They are presumed to be
Daniel Smith and Robert
Sharp and were probably
entered in the missing
volume of Large Workers
marks.

Circa
1769

9 December 1778
with Richard Carter
and Robert Sharp
14 Westmoreland Buildings
Plate workers

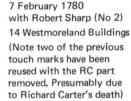

7 February 1780
with Robert Sharp (No 2)
14 Westmoreland Buildings
(Note two of the previous
touch marks have been
reused with the RC part
removed. Presumably due
to Richard Carter's death)

He never became a Freeman of the Goldsmiths' Company.
He was the son of William Smith and was apprenticed to
Thomas Gladwin, a member of the Merchant Taylors'
Company, on 6 November 1740. He obtained his freedom
of that Company on 7 February 1753 and was made a
Liveryman on 25 November 1766. In the Parliamentary
Return of 1773, he and his partner Robert Sharp are
recorded as Plate workers of Aldermanbury.

Smith probably retired or died at the beginning of
January 1788 this being when an old partnership mark
was re-entered by Robert Sharp but with Daniel Smith's
initials removed.

His son George Smith, was apprenticed to Robert
Sharp on 8 May 1765, obtained his freedom on 7
October 1772 and presumably remained with the firm.

William Fountain and Richard Sibley were both
apprenticed to Daniel Smith (Merchant Taylor) and
Fendall Rushforth (Goldsmith) in 1777 and 1785
respectively.

28 February 1731–2
Gutter Lane
Free Goldsmith

4 September 1739
Gutter Lane
Goldsmith

He was the son of George Smith and was apprenticed to
Edmund Peace on 3 March 1704–5. At a later date he
was turned over to John Smith.

He obtained his freedom on 23 May 1718.

George Smith (No 2)

13 December 1750
with Samuel Smith
Foster Lane

He was the son of George Smith (No 1) and was
apprenticed to Gabriel Sleath on 31 December 1728–9.
He obtained his freedom on 7 December 1750.

1 February 1774
110 Wood Street
Spoon maker

12 August 1775
110 Wood Street

23 July 1776
110 Wood Street

22 October 1776
110 Wood Street

20 October 1778
60 Paternoster Row
Spoon maker

17 July 1780
60 Paternoster Row

10 August 1782
60 Paternoster Row

3 November 1786
with William Fearn

60 Paternoster Row

Plate workers

Removed to 1 Lovell's Court,
Paternoster Row, 29 June 1790

From the Goldsmiths' records it seems most probable that
he was the son of Thomas Smith of Wolverhampton,
Staffordshire in which case he was apprenticed to Thomas
Chawner on 4 December 1765 for a period of seven years
to learn the trade of a Spoon maker. At a later date he was
turned over to Pierce Tempest but there is no record of
his having obtained his freedom of the Goldsmiths'
Company. However, there was a George Smith who was
apprenticed about this time to Thomas Chawner's partner,
William Chawner (No 1). As William Chawner was a
member of the Pewterers' Company, this George Smith
became free of the same Company when he obtained his
freedom on 17 March 1768.

Although this was only 2¼ years after George Smith (No
3) was apprenticed to Thomas Chawner, it may well be
that these two Smiths were one and the same person,
having been transferred from one master to another
(i.e. from Thomas to William) during the apprenticeship.
This would explain why no freedom date was recorded
in the Goldsmiths' records and the Pewterers' apprenticeship records no longer exist to verify the supposition.
If there were in fact two George Smiths, it must have
been quite a coincidence to have had both of them
apprenticed to the Chawner firm during the same period
of time.

In the Parliamentary Return of 1773 George Smith was listed as a Spoon maker of 110 Wood Street, so presumably there was an earlier mark than that of 1 February 1774 as illustrated. Probably it was entered in the missing volume of Large Workers' marks from 1759 to 1773.

In 1778 he changed his premises taking over those of his old master Thomas Chawner at 60 Paternoster Row.

During 1786 he entered a mark in partnership with William Fearn, who had been a fellow apprentice with him under Thomas Chawner.

William Fearn entered into partnership with William Eley in 1797 and George Smith (No 3) appears to have retired or died between that year and 1799 when his son George Smith (No 4) entered his own mark from his father's premises.

20 June 1799
1 Lovell Court, Paternoster Row
Spoon maker

8 November 1803
31 St John's Square, Clerkenwell
Spoon maker
Removed to 16 Hosier Lane
Smithfield, 16 February 1807

7 April 1807
with Richard Crossley
Giltspur Street
Spoon makers

20 January 1812
16 Hosier Lane
Spoon maker

He was the son of George Smith (No 3) and was apprenticed
to William Fearn to learn the trade of goldsmith on 5
August 1789. He obtained his freedom on 5 October 1796.
His brother John was apprenticed to William Fearn in
1791, turned over to George (No 4) in 1797 and became
free in 1798.

21 November 1767
Huggin Alley, Wood Street

9 August 1771
Huggin Alley, Wood Street

8 April 1775
4 Huggin Lane
Buckle maker

21 September 1776
4 Huggin Lane

14 May 1778
4 Huggin Lane

27 April 1779
4 Huggin Lane

17 January 1782
4 Huggin Lane

25 January 1782
4 Huggin Lane

G★S
21 December 1782
Huggin Lane

G★S

GS

GS
25 May 1784
Huggin Lane

GS

GS
5 August 1786
4 Huggin Lane

GS
20 March 1787
Huggin Lane

GS

G·S
24 September 1789
Huggin Lane

G·S
Buckle maker

GS
TH
7 January 1792
with Thomas Hayter
4 Huggin Lane

GS
TH
Plate workers

He was the son of George Smith (Yeoman) and was apprenticed on 2 August 1753 to John Eaton and on the same day to Samuel Eaton (Leatherseller of Huggin Court). He obtained his freedom on 14 January 1761, was made a Liveryman in December 1771 and died between 1802 and 1811.

Thomas Hayter was apprenticed to him in 1782 and obtained his freedom in 1790.

George Smith (No 6)

August 1758
Red Cross Street

He was the son of John Smith (Waterman) and was apprenticed to William Aldridge on 2 May 1750. He obtained his freedom on 3 May 1758.

22 April 1718
N.S.
Foster Lane

25 August 1720
O.S.
Foster Lane

He was the son of Thomas Smith and was apprenticed to Peter White on 20 March 1709—10. He obtained his freedom on 3 April 1718 and was made a Liveryman in May 1731. He died in 1737.

John Bayley was apprenticed to him in 1732.

14 September 1744
Winchester Court, Monkwell Street

25 September 1746
Now of Old Bailey

He was the son of James Smith and was apprenticed to John Ferris on 4 September 1735. He was turned over to John Montgomery on 5 December 1738 and obtained his freedom on 5 July 1743.

13 December 1750
with George Smith (No 2)
Foster Lane

4 February 1754
Foster Lane

He was the son of Samuel Smith and was apprenticed to
Samuel Wood on 6 December 1743. He obtained his
freedom on 11 January 1750.

John Spackman (No 1)   S

April 1697
At Charing Cross

He was the son of Thomas Spackman of Marlborough,
Wiltshire, and was apprenticed to Roger Stephens on
15 April 1668. He obtained his freedom of the Goldsmiths' Company on 1 September 1676 and was made
a Liveryman in November 1687.

His brother, Thomas (No 1) was apprenticed to him in
November 1690. Both John (No 2) and Thomas (No 2),
who were possibly his nephews, were apprenticed to him
in 1693 and 1701 respectively. Neither appears to have
obtained his freedom.

11 September 1741
Foster Lane
Goldsmith

24 November 1742
Removed into Gutter Lane
The above mark being lost,
the other mark was entered
at the time of removal.
(The "above mark" refers to
the previous one entered on
11 September 1741).

He was the son of Thomas Spackman (No 1) and was
apprenticed to Elizabeth Goodwin (widow of James)
on 21 October 1730. He was turned over to William
Justice on 29 November 1734 and obtained his freedom
of the Goldsmiths' Company on 6 December 1737.

25 May 1700
Foster Lane

15 January 1706
Foster Lane

1 November 1725
Marlborough

He was the son of Thomas Spackman of Marlborough,
Wiltshire and was apprenticed to William Swadlin and
brother John Spackman (No 1) on 19 November 1690.
He obtained his freedom of the Goldsmiths' Company on
17 May 1700 and was made a Liveryman in October 1708.

He appears to have become bankrupt in 1719 which perhaps
could account for his return to Marlborough before setting
up in business again with a new mark in 1725.

He was dead by October 1730 when his son, John
Spackman (No 3) was apprenticed to Elizabeth Goodwin.

1 November 1714
Lilypot Lane

14 July 1720
O.S.
Lilypot Lane

N.S.

(No date or address.
Marks were entered
between September
1723 and May 1725.)

O.S.

He was the son of Joseph Spackman of Marlborough,
Wiltshire and was apprenticed to William Andrews and
Nathaniel Lock on 27 July 1703. He obtained his freedom
of the Goldsmiths' Company on 4 November 1712.

His two brothers John (No 2) and Thomas (No 2) were
apprenticed to John (No 1) in 1693 and 1701 respectively
but neither appears to have obtained his freedom. It is
possible that both John Spackman (No 1) and Thomas
Spackman (No 1) were his uncles, they being the sons
of Thomas Spackman of Marlborough.

William (No 1) was dead by 7 June 1737 when his son
William (No 2) was apprenticed to goldsmith Robert
Jenkes. William (No 2) was turned over to Peter
Archambo (No 1) on 27 July 1737 and obtained his
freedom of the Goldsmiths' Company on 11 December
1745.

24 July 1729
Foster Lane
Free Goldsmith

15 June 1739
O.S.
Foster Lane

12 December 1739
N.S.
Foster Lane

He was the son of Edward Spilsbury and was apprenticed
to Richard Green on 2 November 1708. He obtained his
freedom on 12 July 1717 and was made a Liveryman in
March 1736.

His son Francis (No 2), obtained his freedom by
Patrimony in 1757, was made a Liveryman in 1763 and
died before 1796.

25 January 1742–3
Compton Street

He was not apprenticed through the Goldsmiths' Company nor was he a Freeman of the Company.

About 1745, he went into partnership with Charles Gouyn (Jeweller) as part manager of the well known Chelsea Porcelain Factory.

From about 1750 to 1756, he was its manager under the patronage of the Duke of Cumberland, Gouyn presumably having severed his connections with the factory.

He then took over as proprietor but in 1757 became very ill and had to close the factory for about a year.

In 1769 he sold out to a James Cox and in 1771, he died.

The factory, meanwhile, had been acquired by William Duesbury of Derby.

2 May 1792
with William Frisbee
5 Cock Lane, Snowhill
Plate workers

12 January 1793
30 Church Street, Soho
Plate worker

27 April 1793
30 Church Street, Soho

8 August 1794
30 Church Street, Soho
Removed to 20 Air Street,
St James, 8 October 1796

29 November 1799
20 Air Street, Piccadilly

21 August 1807
53 Dean Street, Soho
Plate worker

18 February 1808
53 Dean Street, Soho
Plate worker

15 December 1808
53 Dean Street, Soho

21 October 1813
53 Dean Street, Soho

12 September 1817
53 Dean Street, Soho
Plate worker

Removed to Harrison Street,
Grays Inn Road,
4 March 1819

2 September 1833
17 Harrison Street,
Grays Inn Road
Plate worker

17 December 1834
17 Harrison Street

Born in 1771, he was the son of Thomas Storr, a silver chaser, who became a victualler. About 1785, he was apprenticed to the Swedish silversmith, Andrew Fogelberg of 30 Church Street, Soho. In 1792 he completed his apprenticeship but never became a freeman of the Goldsmiths' Company.

On 2 May 1792, he entered his first mark in partnership with William Frisbee. This partnership did not last long for Storr entered his own mark on 12 January 1793 having taken over Fogelberg's premises at Church Street. By October 1796 he had moved to 20 Air Street, Piccadilly.

In 1801 he married Elizabeth Susanna Beyer, the daughter of a family of pianoforte and organ builders in Compton Street. She was a year older than Paul Storr. They had ten children, seven girls and three boys. Elizabeth born in 1802, Harriet in 1804, Paul in 1805, Emma in 1806, Francis in 1808, Mary Anne in 1809, Eleanor in 1811, Sophia in 1812, John Bridge in 1814 and Anna Maria in 1815. In spite of Storr's large family there was no son to carry on the business when he retired.

Paul junior joined the Merchant Service when about 14 years old and became a sailor while Francis, having spent about five years working with his father from 1824 to 1829, decided to take holy orders. This he attained by going to Queens College, Oxford in 1829 where he took his B.A. in 1833 and his M.A. degree in 1836.

His third son, John Bridge, so named after one of Storr's business partners in Rundell, Bridge and Rundell, unfortunately died while still an infant.

In 1807, Storr was persuaded to take over the manufacturing side of Rundell, Bridge and Rundell. This branch of the firm was called "Storr and Co" with workshops at 53 Dean Street, while the parent company, run by Philip Rundell and John Bridge, was the retail outlet for the workshop's products.

Although Storr always stamped his own mark on his silverware, Rundell, Bridge and Rundell often added their mark elsewhere on the article. Theirs was not entered at the Goldsmiths' Hall.

By 1811, Storr was a partner in the firm, the other partners being Philip Rundell, John Bridge, Edmund Rundell and William Theed. Storr liked John Bridge but could not get on with quarrelsome Philip Rundell. Eventually this caused Storr to leave the firm and open his own workshop at 18 Harrison Street off Grays Inn Road in March 1819.

In 1822, Storr took over a shop at 13 New Bond Street as a retail outlet for his goods. It was run for him by John Mortimer who had been an assistant of Mr. Gray, the previous owner. Meanwhile Storr continued running the workshop in Harrison Street. The firm was called "Storr and Mortimer, Goldsmiths and Silversmiths".

By 1826 trade had dwindled and Mortimer had so overstocked the shop that they were nearly bankrupt.

Storr then appealed to John Samuel Hunt, his nephew by marriage for assistance. The result was that Hunt became a partner by bringing £5,000 into the firm. The firm thus continued until 1838 when it moved to 156 New Bond Street.

Storr and Mortimer however, were constantly having
disputes and eventually in 1838, Storr retired with his
wife to Hill House, Tooting where she died on 4 November
1843 and he died on 18 March 1844.

Mary Sumner

---

   18 March 1807
                        1 Clerkenwell Close
                        Spoon maker

   31 August 1809
                        with Elizabeth Sumner
                        1 Clerkenwell Close
                        Spoon makers

   21 August 1810
                        with Elizabeth Sumner
                        1 Clerkenwell Close

Probably she was the wife of William Sumner (No 1) and
took over the family business when William died in 1807.
Elizabeth Sumner was probably their daughter.

1 May 1775
with Richard Crossley
1 Clerkenwell Close
Plate workers

27 January 1776
with Richard Crossley
1 Clerkenwell Close

1 May 1777
with Richard Crossley
1 Clerkenwell Close

27 January 1780
with Richard Crossley
1 Clerkenwell Close

6 April 1782
1 Clerkenwell Close
Plate worker

14 December 1784
1 Clerkenwell Close
Spoon maker

9 May 1787
1 Clerkenwell Close
Spoon maker

7 June 1788
1 Clerkenwell Close

30 September 1799
1 Clerkenwell Close

15 October 1802
1 Clerkenwell Close
Spoon maker

31 March 1803
1 Clerkenwell Close

He was the son of Gilbert Sumner and was apprenticed to
Thomas Chawner on 5 October 1763. He obtained his
freedom on 7 November 1770, was made a Liveryman
in February 1791 and presumably died in 1807 when
Mary Sumner entered her mark.

She was probably his wife.

12 May 1787
9 Albion Buildings,
Bartholomew Close
Small worker

He was not apprenticed through the Goldsmiths' Company
nor was he a Freeman of the Company.

Possibly he was a relative of William Sumner (No 1).

John Sutton

15 April 1697
Lombard Street
Present Touchwarden

He was the son of Thomas Sutton and was apprenticed to
John Winterton on 8 February 1660—61.

At a later date he was turned over to Arthur Manwaring.

He obtained his freedom on 19 February 1667 and was
made a Liveryman in September 1674. He became 4th
Warden in 1696, 3rd Warden in 1701, 2nd Warden in
1703 and Prime Warden in 1707.

In 1697 he was the Company's Touch Warden.

His brother, Leonard, was apprenticed to him on 26
August 1668 and obtained his freedom on 27 October
1675.

7 January 1711–12
Mugwell Street

He was the son of Charles Sutton (Butcher) and was apprenticed to John Ladyman (Goldsmith) on 29 September 1702. He obtained his freedom of the Goldsmiths' Company on 5 December 1711.

(No date) (Entered between May and October 1728)
Staning Lane   Goldsmith

29 June 1739
Noble Street Goldsmith

18 July 1757
Noble Street

22 August 1757
Noble Street

He was the son of Anthony Swift (Merchant Taylor) and was apprenticed to Thomas Langford (goldsmith) on 6 March 1717. He was turned over to William Paradise (goldsmith) on 6 April 1719 and later turned over to Thomas Tearle (goldsmith) on 9 May 1723. He obtained his freedom of the Goldsmiths' Company on 10 June 1725 and was made a Liveryman in March 1758.

His son, John, was apprenticed to him in 1750 and
obtained his freedom of the Goldsmiths' Company in
1758.

Richard Syng

April 1697
In Carey Lane

April 1697
In Carey Lane

He was the son of George Syng and was apprenticed to
Abraham Hinde on 2 April 1679. He obtained his
freedom on 23 November 1687 and was made a Liveryman in April 1705.

His two sons Benjamin and Joseph were apprenticed to
him in 1709 and 1711 respectively. There is no record
of Benjamin obtaining his freedom, but Joseph obtained
his by Patrimony in 1734.

Circa 1726
O.S.
Green Street,
near Leicester Fields

Circa 1726
N.S.
Green Street,
near Leicester Fields

She was the wife of David Tanqueray and the daughter of
David Willaume (No 1) to whom her husband had been
apprenticed.

When her husband died circa 1726, she took over the
family business and entered her own mark.

She was dead by January 1737—8 when one of her
apprentices obtained his freedom.

23 December 1713
N.S.

Green Street,
near Leicester Fields

12 August 1720
O.S.

Green Street,
near Leicester Fields

He was the son of David Tanqueray of the Province of Normandy, France and was apprenticed to David Willaume (No 1) on 16 September 1708.

He entered his first mark in December 1713 after only five years apprenticeship. Eventually he took up his freedom of the Goldsmiths' Company on 4 October 1722.

His wife Ann, was the daughter of David Willaume; presumably they met when he was an apprentice in Willaume's workshop.

He was dead by January 1726—7 when one of his apprentices was turned over to his widow.

3 May 1744
Maiden Lane, Wood Street

27 January 1757
Maiden Lane, Wood Street

He was the son of Thomas Taylor and was apprenticed to
John Newton on 3 March 1736—37. He obtained his
freedom on 3 April 1744 and was made a Liveryman in
May 1751.

In the Parliamentary Return of 1773 he was recorded as
a Plate worker of Maiden Lane.

James Tookey

11 May 1750
Noble Street, Foster Lane

He was the son of Charles Tookey and was apprenticed to
Henry Green on 5 April 1733. He obtained his freedom on
2 July 1741 and was made a Liveryman in March 1758.

He was not recorded in the Parliamentary Return of 1773
but an Elizabeth Tookey was recorded as a spoon maker
of Silver Street. Possibly she was James' wife and had
recently taken over the family business following James'
death.

His son Thomas, was apprenticed to him in 1766 and
obtained his freedom in 1773.

7 January 1740—1
George Street, York Buildings

Presumably she was the wife of John Tuite and entered
her mark in January 1741 following her husband's death.

1720

Irelands Yard in Blackfriars

Removed to Litchfield Street
near Newport Market

Circa 1733   (These two marks are not
               recorded at Goldsmiths' Hall.
               Possibly J. Tuite did not
               enter them as they are similar

Circa 1732   to his first entry of 1720.)

27 June 1739

Litchfield Street
St Anns, Westminster

He was the son of James Tuite of Drogheda, Ireland and
in 1703 was apprenticed to John Matthews, a goldsmith
in Dublin. He obtained his freedom in 1710 and came
to London in 1720.

He may have died in December 1740 since Elizabeth
Tuite, who was probably his wife, entered a mark of her
own in January 1741.

1756
Kings Street, Golden Square

He was not apprenticed through the Goldsmiths' Company
nor was he a freeman of the Company.

Possibly he was the son of John and Elizabeth Tuite.

In the Parliamentary Return of 1773 he was recorded as
a Plate worker of Great Queen Street, Lincoln's Inn.

Walter Tweedie

7 December 1775
Holywell Street, Strand
Spoon maker

29 October 1781
Holywell Street, Strand

25 September 1779
5 Holywell Street, Strand

Plate worker

He was not apprenticed through the Goldsmiths' Company
nor was he a Freeman of the Company.

In the Parliamentary Return of 1773 he was recorded as a
Spoon maker of Holywell Street, so presumably an earlier
mark was entered in one of the missing records.

18 June 1739
Green Street, Leicester Fields

He was the son of John Vedeau and was apprenticed to
David Willaume (No 2) on 3 May 1723. He obtained his
freedom on 8 January 1733 and was made a Liveryman
in September 1746.

In the Parliamentary Return of 1773 he was recorded as
a Plate worker of Green Street, Leicester Fields.

In July 1742, he and five other members resigned from
the Goldsmiths' Company in order to be independent
witnesses for the prosecution at the trial of six goldsmiths
charged with counterfeiting assay marks on wrought plate
to avoid paying duty and assay charges. The six accused
were:- Richard Gosling, Edward Aldridge, James Smith,
David Mowden, Louis Laroche and Matthias Standfast.
Of these six, it seems that only Edward Aldridge was
acquitted, the others being fined or jailed.

On 5 August 1742, following the completion of his
evidence, Aymé Vedeau was re-elected into the Goldsmiths' Company.

25 June 1739
Dean Street, Fetter Lane

He was the son of Robert Vincent and was apprenticed to
William Parker on 17 December 1711.
On 13 December 1716, he was turned over to George
Wanley.
He obtained his freedom on 3 December 1719.

17 November 1747
Panton Street, near Haymarket

        Circa
        1759

This mark is not recorded at
Goldsmiths' Hall. Possibly
John Parker and Edward
Wakelin. It may have been
entered in the missing volume
of Large Workers marks.

He was the son of Edward Wakelin and was apprenticed to
John Le Sage on 3 June 1730. He eventually took up his
freedom on 7 September 1748. In 1747, he became a
partner in George Wickes's firm.

In the Parliamentary Return of 1773 he and his partner
John Parker were recorded as Goldsmiths of Panton
Street. John was the son of Thomas Parker (Gentleman)
and had been apprenticed to George Wickes on 5 July
1751.

Edward Wakelin probably retired about 1776 and died in
1784. His son John, was apprenticed to him in 1766.

25 September 1776
with William Taylor
Panton Street
Plate workers

9 May 1777
with William Taylor
Panton Street

20 October 1792
with Robert Garrard
Panton Street
Plate workers

He was the son of Edward Wakelin and was apprenticed
to his father on 5 March 1766. He eventually took up his
freedom by Patrimony on 6 January 1779 and appears to
have retired or died in 1802 when Robert Garrard
entered his own mark.

8 March 1758
Little Brittain

 7 November 1778
* Monkwell Street
 Plate worker

 6 January 1780
* 54 Red Lion Street, Clerkenwell
Buckle maker
 ⊕ 26 October 1786 (Address as before)

 16 July 1787 (Address as before)

 ⊕ 26 June 1789 (Address as before)

 ⊕ 15 September 1792
54 Red Lion Street, Clerkenwell
Plate worker
 ⊕ 16 August 1796 (Address as before)

 ⊕ 14 September 1801 (Address as before)

22 February 1810
with Jonathan Hayne

 16 Red Lion Street, Clerkenwell
Plate workers

 * 3 December 1817
(Address as before)

 17 February 1820
(Address as before)

He was the son of John Wallis and was apprenticed to
William Jones on 7 June 1749. He obtained his freedom
on 1 December 1756, was made a Liveryman in December
1771 and died either in 1820 or 1821.

In the Parliamentary Return of 1773 he was recorded as a
Plate worker of 37 Monkwell Street.

Jonathan Hayne was apprenticed to him in 1796 and
obtained his freedom in 1804.

⊕ Mark entered in two sizes
* Mark entered in three sizes.

April 1697
Water Lane near Fleet Street

19 September 1717
St Paul's Churchyard

He was the son of John Ward and was apprenticed to his
father on 26 March 1684—5. He obtained his freedom
on 29 May 1692, was made a Liveryman in April 1705 and
an Assistant in October 1714.

In 1723 he became bankrupt and resigned from the
Goldsmiths' Company in January 1726.

10 February 1709—10
N.S.
Maiden Lane

24 June 1720
O.S.
Gutter Lane

He was the son of William Watts and was apprenticed to Christopher Canner (No 1) on 8 December 1698. He obtained his freedom on 17 March 1707.

He was dead by 6 May 1736 when his son Joseph was apprenticed to John Fessey. Joseph obtained his freedom of the Goldsmiths' Company on 7 June 1743.

11 May 1756
Maiden Lane, Wood Street

20 April 1757
Maiden Lane, Wood Street

He was the son of William Wheat and was apprenticed to
Henry Bickerton on 3 September 1746. He obtained his
freedom on 7 April 1756. In Parliamentary Return of 1773
he is recorded as a Goldsmith of Maiden Lane.

Samuel Wheatley

27 April 1810
with John Evans
3 Old Street, Goswell Street
Plate workers

23 August 1811
3 Old Street, St Lukes
Plate worker

He was the son of James Wheatley and was apprenticed to
Ann Chesterman on 5 April 1777.

On 5 April 1780 he was turned over to Charles Chesterman
by consent of Sarah Chesterman the executor of Ann's
will.

He obtained his freedom on 5 May 1784.

20 June 1737
Foster Lane
Free Goldsmith

18 June 1739
Foster Lane

1 May 1740
with William Williams
Foster Lane
Removed to Ave Maria Lane
25 July 1753

24 October 1757
with Charles Wright
Ave Maria Lane

Circa
1759

This mark is not recorded
at Goldsmiths' Hall.
Possibly Thomas Whipham and
Charles Wright. May have been
entered in the missing volume
of Large Workers marks.

He was the son of William Whipham and was apprenticed to Thomas Farren on 3 July 1728.

He obtained his freedom on 7 June 1737, was made a Liveryman in September 1746 and an Assistant in 1752.

He became 4th Warden in 1765, 3rd Warden in 1766, 2nd Warden in 1767, and Prime Warden in 1771.

In the Parliamentary Return of 1773, he was listed as a Goldsmith of Fleet Street. His son, Thomas, obtained his freedom by Patrimony in 1768 and eventually became Prime Warden in 1790. This is one of the rare cases where both father and son became Prime Wardens of the Goldsmiths' Company.

Thomas junior continued to work as a partner in the firm with his father and Charles Wright.

Charles Wright was apprenticed to Thomas Whipham senior in 1747.

31 December 1744
Golden Ball & Pearl,
Noble Street

4 March 1744—5
with John Fray
Golden Ball & Pearl,
Noble Street

9 January 1750
Golden Ball & Pearl,
Noble Street

5 July 1758
Golden Ball & Pearl,
Noble Street

He was the son of Fuller White and was apprenticed to
Edward Feline on 8 January 1733—34. He obtained his
freedom on 5 December 1744, was made a Liveryman
in March 1750 and died on 2 July 1775.

In Parliamentary Return of 1773 he was recorded as a
Plate worker of Noble Street.

10 December 1719
N.S.

At the corner of Arundel Street
in the Strand

4 January 1724—25
O.S.

At the corner of Arundel Street,
in the Strand

26 June 1739

At corner of Green Street,
near Leicester Fields

He was the son of Christopher White and was apprenticed
to Robert Cooper on 8 September 1711. He obtained his
freedom on 3 December 1719.

3 February 1721–22
N.S.

3 February 1721–22
O.S.
Threadneedle Street

30 June 1735
Panton Street, St James,
Haymarket

6 July 1739
Kings Arms, Panton Street,
near Haymarket

He was the son of James Wickes and was apprenticed to
Samuel Wastell on 2 December 1712. He obtained his
freedom on 16 June 1720 and was made a Liveryman in
March 1739. He appears to have died about 1770. In 1747,
Edward Wakelin joined him as a partner and entered his
own mark.

April 1697
St James Street

29 January 1718–19
St James Street

27 July 1720
O.S.
St James Street

He was the son of Adam Willaume and trained as a silver-smith in Metz, France. He came to England in 1686 as a Huguenot refugee where he took out papers of denization in 1687. In 1690 he married Marie Mettayer and in 1693, Louis Mettayer (probably her brother) was apprenticed to him.

On 27 January 1693, by order of the Court of Aldermen of the City of London, he was made a Freeman of the Goldsmiths' Company by Redemption.

351

He was made a Liveryman in 1698 and an Assistant in 1724.
In 1700, both Pierre Le Cheaube and Jean Petry were
apprenticed to him while in 1706 his own son David (No 2)
was apprenticed to him. In 1708, David Tanqueray was
apprenticed to him and eventually married his daughter
Ann Willaume. Both Willaume senior and junior kept "running cashes" which was a system of lending money on security.
Willaume (No 1) probably died at some date prior to April
1728, this being when his son entered his own mark from
from the same address.

David Willaume (No 2)

 2 April 1728
N.S.

 2 April 1728
O.S.

St James of St George,
Hanover Square

 19 June 1739
(No address given)

He was the son of David Willaume (No 1) and was
apprenticed to his father on 6 March 1706. He eventually
took up his freedom by Patrimony on 2 May 1723 and
was made a Liveryman in March 1726. His sister Ann
married David Tanqueray.

Aymé Vedeau was apprenticed to Willaume (No 2) on
3 May 1723, the day after he obtained his own freedom.

William Cripps was apprenticed to him in 1730.

1st May 1740
with Thomas Whipham
Foster Lane
Goldsmiths

10 September 1742
Spread Eagle, Foster Lane

He was the son of William Williams and was apprenticed to
Thomas Farren on 9 September 1731. He obtained his
freedom on 5 December 1738 and was made a Liveryman
in September 1746.

Joseph Willmore

21 February 1805
14 Bouverie Street, Fleet Street
Small worker
Removed to 11 Thavies Inn,
Holborn, 6 March 1823

14 March 1840
(No address. Presumably
11 Thavies Inn)

He was not apprenticed through the Goldsmiths' Company
nor was he a Freeman of the Company.

N.S.

18 August 1722

On Puddledock Hill
at the end of
Great Carter Lane

O.S.

26 August 1735
Carey Lane

30 September 1740
Carey Lane

He was the son of John Wood (Turner) and was apprenticed to James Roode (Goldsmith) on 6 July 1715.

He obtained his freedom of the Goldsmiths' Company on 2 August 1722.

David Hennell (No 1) was apprenticed to him in 1728.

3 July 1733
Gutter Lane by Cheapside

29 September 1737
Gutter Lane by Cheapside
Free Goldsmith

15 June 1739
Gutter Lane
Removed to Foster Lane
15 July 1754

24 October 1756
Foster Lane

He was the son of George Wood and was apprenticed to
Thomas Bamford on 7 June 1721. He obtained his freedom on 5 March 1730, was made a Liveryman in March
1737 and an Assistant in 1745. He became 4th Warden in
1758, 3rd Warden in 1759, 2nd Warden in 1760 and
Prime Warden in 1763.

24 October 1757
with Thomas Whipham
Ave Maria Lane

Circa 1759
This mark is not recorded at Goldsmiths' Hall. Possibly Thomas Whipham and Charles Wright. May have been entered in the missing volume of Large Workers marks.

22 July 1775
9 Ave Maria Lane
Plate worker

3 February 1780
9 Ave Maria Lane

25 August 1780
9 Ave Maria Lane

He was the son of a Thomas Wright and was apprenticed to Thomas Whipham on 3 June 1747. He obtained his freedom on 3 July 1754, was made a Liveryman in 1758 and an Assistant in 1777. He became 4th Warden in 1783, 3rd Warden in 1784 and 2nd Warden in 1785. He resigned in 1790 and died in 1815.

Edward Barnard (No 1) and Henry Nutting were apprenticed to him in 1781 and 1782 respectively.

6 September 1721
O.S.
Maiden Lane

He was the son of John Wright and obtained his freedom
by Patrimony on 3 December 1719.

Thomas Wright (No 2)

12 August 1774
Jewin Court, Jewin Street
Buckle maker

27 April 1778
Jewin Court, Jewin Street
Later removed to 10 Great Turnstile,
Holborn
Removed to 30 Little Bell Alley,
Coleman Street, 17 February 1802.

He was not apprenticed through the Goldsmiths' Company
nor was he a Freeman of the Company.

LONDON HALLMARKS

 Standard Mark (Lion Passant)

Denotes a minimum silver content of 92.5%. This mark (for Sterling Standard silver) is used by all Assay Offices in England. It has been struck on English silverware since 1544.

 Britannia Mark

Denotes a minimum silver content of 95.84%. This mark (for Britannia Standard silver) was introduced in 1697 and remained in compulsory use until 1720 when the Sterling Standard was restored. The Britannia Standard continues as an optional alternative and is still used occasionally.

 Assay Office Mark (or Town Mark)

This indicates the Assay Office at which the assaying and hallmarking were carried out. The Leopard's Head mark illustrated here represents the London Assay Office and appears on articles of gold and Sterling Standard silver.

The mark is often found on provincial silver where it appears in addition to the provincial town mark.

Since 1820, the London Assay Office has used an uncrowned Leopard's Head.

Lion's Head Erased

This is an Assay Office Mark used in conjunction with
the Britannia mark on articles of Britannia Standard. In
the London Assay Office, it replaced the Leopard's Head
as Town mark when the Britannia Standard was introduced
in 1697, but in other English Assay Offices, it was used
together with the appropriate Town mark.

 Sovereign's Head (or Duty Mark)

This indicates that excise duty was paid on the article of
gold or silverware bearing it. The duty was collected by
the Assay Office on behalf of the Commissioners of
Stamps (later the Inland Revenue).

The mark was introduced in 1784 and remained in use
until 1890 when the duty was abolished.

 Date Letter Mark

This indicates the year in which the article was hallmarked.
At the London Assay Office, this mark is changed during
May each year, thus each Date Letter covers a portion of
two calender years.

A twenty letter alphabet is always used by the London
Assay Office.

'Drawback' Mark

This mark was in use for less than eight months, from
1 December 1784 to 24 July 1785. The mark constitutes
an incuse figure depicting Britannia and was stamped by
the Assay Office on articles intended for export.

Normally a manufacturer paid excise duty to the Assay
Office on all articles as they were assayed at a rate of
8s per ounce on gold and 6d per ounce on silver. When a
manufacturer later specified that an article was to be
exported, the duty was 'drawn back' and repaid to him,
this transaction being indicated on the finished article
by the incuse Britannia mark.

The procedure was abandoned after such a short period
because stamping the mark on a finished article could
cause damage, although the manufacturer continued to
be reimbursed for the duty he had paid on the article
that was to be exported.

1678

 1688
William
Mary

 1679

 1689

 1680

1690

 1681

1691

 1682

1692

 1683

1693

 1684

James II

1694

William III

 1685

1695

 1686

1696
To
26 March
1697

 1687

1697 { 27 March
to
29 May

 1706

 1697

 1707

 1698

 1708

 1699

 1709

1700

 1710

1701
Anne

1711

1702

 1712

1703

 1713
George I

 1704

1714

 1705

 1715

 **A** 1716

 L 1726
George I

B 1717

M 1727

C 1718

N 1728

   D 1719   **O** 1729

E 1720

P 1730

F 1721

Q 1731

G 1722

R 1732

H 1723

S 1733

I 1724

T 1734

 **K** 1725

V 1735

363

		a	1736		i	1746
		b	1737		m	1747
		C	1738		n	1748
		d	1739		o	1749
		d	1739		p	1750
		e	1740		q	1751
		f	1741		r	1752
		g	1742		ſ	1753
		h	1743		t	1754
		i	1744		u	1755
		k	1745			

A 1756	L 1766
B 1757	M 1767
C 1758	N 1768
D 1759	O 1769
George III	
E 1760	P 1770
F 1761	Q 1771
G 1762	R 1772
H 1763	S 1773
I 1764	T 1774
K 1765	U 1775

365

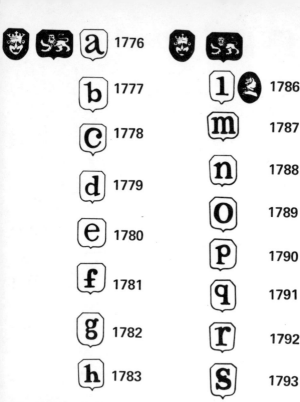

		a 1776
		b 1777
		c 1778
		d 1779
		e 1780
		f 1781
		g 1782
		h 1783
	i 1784	
		k 1785

l 1786	
m 1787	
n 1788	
o 1789	
p 1790	
q 1791	
r 1792	
s 1793	
t 1794	
u 1795	

 **A** 1796

L 1806

B 1797

M 1807

C 1798

N 1808

D 1799

O 1809

E 1800

P 1810

F 1801

Q 1811

G 1802

R 1812

H 1803

S 1813

I 1804

T 1814

K 1805

U 1815

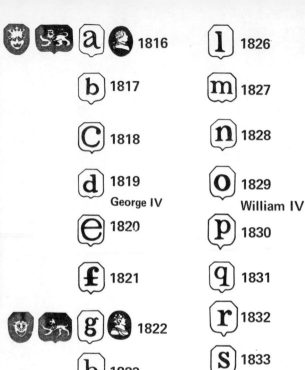

 a **1816**

b 1817

C 1818

d 1819
George IV

e 1820

f 1821

 g **1822**

h 1823

i 1824 t **1834**

k 1825

l 1826

m 1827

n 1828

o 1829
William IV

p 1830

q 1831

r 1832

s 1833

u 1835

		A	1836 Victoria	**L** 1846
		B	1837	**M** 1847
		C	1838	**N** 1848
		D	1839	**O** 1849
		E	1840	**P** 1850
		F	1841	**Q** 1851
		G	1842	**R** 1852
		H	1843	**S** 1853
		J	1844	**T** 1854
		K	1845	**U** 1855

 1856

 1857

 1858

 1859

 1860

 1861

 1862

 1863

 1864

 1865

 1866

 1867

 1868

 1869

 1870

 1871

 1872

 1873

 1874

 1875

 1876

 1886

 1877

 1887

 1878

 1888

 1879

 1889

 1880

 1890
Queen's head
not used after
1890

 1881

 1882

 1891

 1892

 1893

1894

 1895

371

a 1896	**1** 1906
b 1897	**m** 1907
c 1898	**n** 1908
d 1899	**o** 1909 George V
e 1900	**p** 1910
Edward VII **f** 1901	**q** 1911
g 1902	**r** 1912
h 1903	**s** 1913
i 1904	**t** 1914
k 1905	**u** 1915

	a 1916		**l** 1926
	b 1917		**m** 1927
	c 1918		**n** 1928
	d 1919		**o** 1929
	e 1920		**p** 1930
	f 1921		**q** 1931
	g 1922		**r** 1932
 **h** 1923			**s** 1933
	i 1924		**t** 1934
	k 1925		**u** 1935

Edward VIII

373

1936

George VI

 1946

 1937

 1947

1938

1948

 1939

 1949

 1940

1950

 1941

1951

Elizabeth II

 1942

 1952

 1943

 1953

 1944

 1954

1945

 1955

374

a 1956	**l** 1966
b 1957	**m** 1967
c 1958	**n** 1968
d 1959	**o** 1969
e 1960	**p** 1970
f 1961	
g 1962	
h 1963	
i 1964	
k 1965	

A

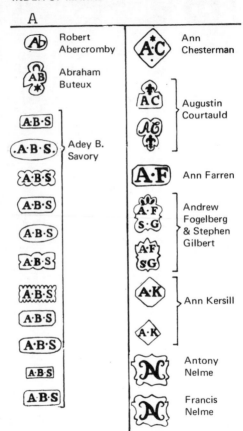

	Robert Abercromby
	Abraham Buteux
A·B·S	
·A·B·S·	
A·B·S	
A·B·S	Adey B. Savory
A·B·S	
A·B·S	
A·B·S	
A·B·S	
A·B·S	
A·B·S	
A·B·S	

A·C	Ann Chesterman
AC	
AC	Augustin Courtauld
A·F	Ann Farren
A·F S·G	
A·F sG	Andrew Fogelberg & Stephen Gilbert
A·K	
A·K	Ann Kersill
N	Antony Nelme
N	Francis Nelme

Abraham L. De Oliveyra

 Peter Archambo (No 1)

 Adey, Joseph, & Albert Savory

 Ann Smith & Nathaniel Appleton

Ann Tanqueray

Ayme Videau

B

 Mary Bainbridge

 William Bainbridge

Thomas Bamford

 John Bache

 Richard Bayley

 Benjamin Cartwright (No 1)

 Benjamin Cartwright (No 2)

377

Benjamin
Cartwright
(No 2)

 William
Bellassyse

 Benjamin
Gignac

 ⎤
⎥ Benjamin
⎥ Godfrey
 ⎦

 ⎤
⎥
⎥ Joseph
⎥ Bird
⎥
⎦

 John
Boddington

 Benjamin
Smith
(No 1)

 ⎤
⎥
⎥ Benjamin
⎥ Smith (No 1)
⎥ & James
⎥ Smith
⎦

 ⎤
⎥ Benjamin
⎥ Smith
⎥ (No 1)
⎦

 ⎤
⎥ Benjamin
 ⎥ Smith (No 1) &
⎥ Benjamin
⎥ Smith
⎥ (No 2)
⎦

 ⎤
⎥ Benjamin
 ⎦ Smith
(No 2)

378

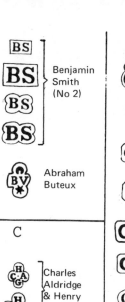

BS
BS
BS
BS
} Benjamin Smith (No 2)

Abraham Buteux

C

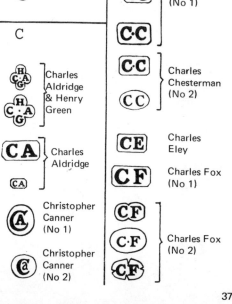

H
C·A
G
C·A
H
G
} Charles Aldridge & Henry Green

CA
CA
} Charles Aldridge

CA — Christopher Canner (No 1)

Ca — Christopher Canner (No 2)

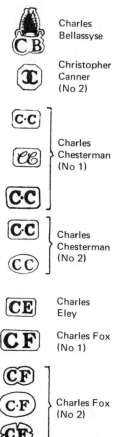

Charles Bellassyse

CB

Christopher Canner (No 2)

C·C
CC
CC
} Charles Chesterman (No 1)

C·C
CC
} Charles Chesterman (No 2)

CE — Charles Eley

CF — Charles Fox (No 1)

CF
C·F
CF
} Charles Fox (No 2)

Charles Fox (No 2)

 Crispin Fuller

 John Chartier

 Pierre Le Cheaube

 Charles Kandler (No 1)

 Charles Kandler (No 2)

 Joseph Clare (No 1)

 Joseph Clare (No 2)

 Nicholas Clausen

 Lawrence Coles

 Matthew Cooper

 Robert Cooper

 Isaac Cornasseau

 Edward Cornock

380

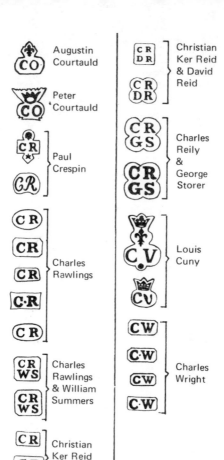

Augustin Courtauld

Peter Courtauld

Paul Crespin

Charles Rawlings

Charles Rawlings & William Summers

Christian Ker Reid

Christian Ker Reid & David Reid

Charles Reily & George Storer

Louis Cuny

Charles Wright

D

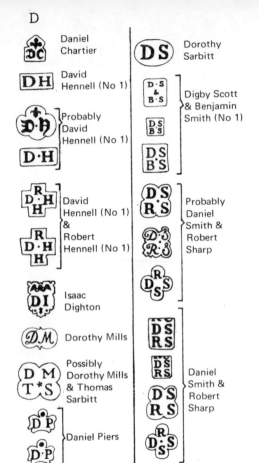

Daniel Chartier	Dorothy Sarbitt
David Hennell (No 1)	Digby Scott & Benjamin Smith (No 1)
Probably David Hennell (No 1)	
David Hennell (No 1) & Robert Hennell (No 1)	Probably Daniel Smith & Robert Sharp
Isaac Dighton	
Dorothy Mills	
Possibly Dorothy Mills & Thomas Sarbitt	Daniel Smith & Robert Sharp
Daniel Piers	

382

David
Tanqueray

 David
Willaume
(No 1)

 David
Willaume
(No 2)

E

 Edward
Aldridge

 Edward
Aldridge
& John
Stamper

 Edward
Edward Jnr,
John &
William
Barnard

 Edward,
Edward Junior,
John &
William
Barnard

 Edmund
Boddington

 Elizabeth
Buteux

 Ebenezer
Coker

 Edward
Cornock

 John
Eckford
(No 1)

 Edward
Edwards

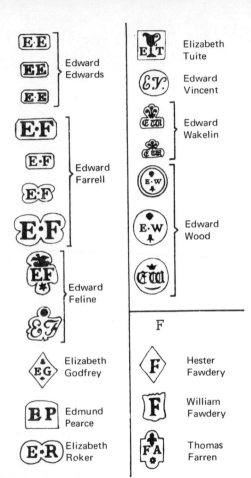

E·E	Edward Edwards
EE	
E·E	
E·F	Edward Farrell
E·F	
E·F	
E·F	
EF	Edward Feline
EF	
EG	Elizabeth Godfrey
BP	Edmund Pearce
E·R	Elizabeth Roker

ET	Elizabeth Tuite
EV	Edward Vincent
EW	Edward Wakelin
EW	
E·W	Edward Wood
E·W	
EW	

F

F	Hester Fawdery
F	William Fawdery
FA	Thomas Farren

John Fawdery (No 1)

 William Fawdery

 Francis Crump (No 1)

 Edward Feline

 Francis Harache

 Charles F. Kandler

 Charles F. Kandler

 William Fleming

 Francis Nelme

 Thomas Folkingham

 William Fordham

 James Fraillon

 Francis Spilsbury

 Fuller White

385

Fuller White

G

 Daniel Garnier

 Francis Garthorne

 George Garthorne

 George Baskerville

 George Baskerville & William Sampel

 George Baskerville & Thomas Morley

 George Heming & William Chawner (No 1)

 George Hindmarsh

 James Gould

 William Gould

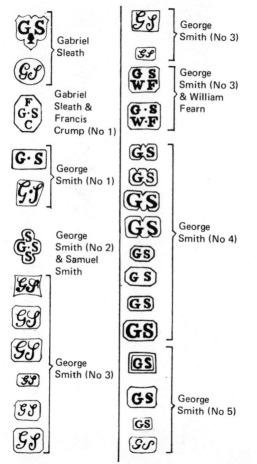

Gabriel Sleath

Gabriel Sleath & Francis Crump (No 1)

George Smith (No 1)

George Smith (No 2) & Samuel Smith

George Smith (No 3)

George Smith (No 3)

George Smith (No 3) & William Fearn

George Smith (No 4)

George Smith (No 5)

George
Smith (No 6)

  John P.
Guerier

  George
Wickes

 George
Smith
(No 5)

H

  Paul
Hanet

 George
Smith (No 5)
& Thomas
Hayter

 Pierre
Harache
(No 1)

Pierre
Harache
(No 2)

388

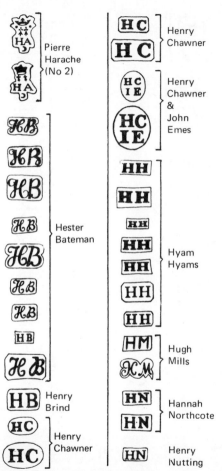

Pierre Harache (No 2)

Hester Bateman

Henry Brind

Henry Chawner

Henry Chawner

Henry Chawner & John Emes

Hyam Hyams

Hugh Mills

Hannah Northcote

Henry Nutting

13

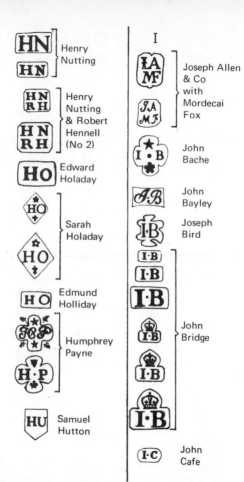

HN
HN — Henry Nutting

HN RH
HN RH — Henry Nutting & Robert Hennell (No 2)

HO — Edward Holaday

HO
HO — Sarah Holaday

HO — Edmund Holliday

HP
HP — Humphrey Payne

HU — Samuel Hutton

I

IA MF
IA MF — Joseph Allen & Co with Mordecai Fox

I·B — John Bache

J·B — John Bayley

IB — Joseph Bird

I·B
I·B
I·B
IB
IB
I·B — John Bridge

I·C — John Cafe

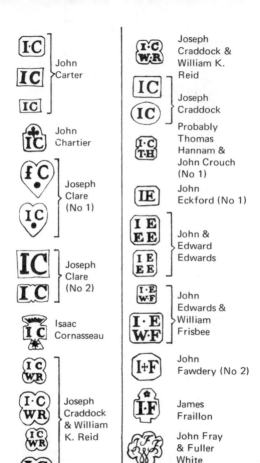

John Carter

John Chartier

Joseph Clare (No 1)

Joseph Clare (No 2)

Isaac Cornasseau

Joseph Craddock & William K. Reid

Joseph Craddock & William K. Reid

Joseph Craddock

Probably Thomas Hannam & John Crouch (No 1)

John Eckford (No 1)

John & Edward Edwards

John Edwards & William Frisbee

John Fawdery (No 2)

James Fraillon

John Fray & Fuller White

391

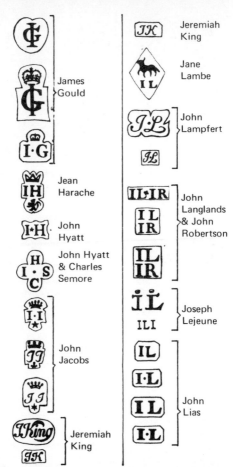

James Gould

Jean Harache

John Hyatt

John Hyatt & Charles Semore

John Jacobs

Jeremiah King

Jeremiah King

Jane Lambe

John Lampfert

John Langlands & John Robertson

Joseph Lejeune

John Lias

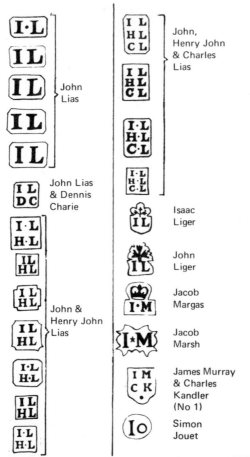

I·L

IL

IL   John
Lias
IL

IL

I L
D C   John Lias
& Dennis
Charie

I·L
H·L

IL
HL

I L
HL   John &
Henry John
Lias
I L
HL

I·L
H·L

IL
HL

I·L
H·L

I L
H L
C L   John,
Henry John
& Charles
Lias
I L
H L
C

I·L·
H·L·
C·L·

I·L·
H·L·
C·L·

IL   Isaac
Liger

IL   John
Liger

I·M   Jacob
Margas

I·M   Jacob
Marsh

I M
C K·   James Murray
& Charles
Kandler
(No 1)

Io   Simon
Jouet

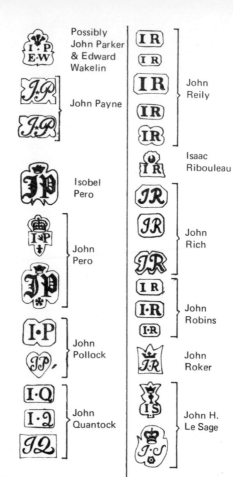

Mark	Maker
I · P / E · W	Possibly John Parker & Edward Wakelin
J.P (×2)	John Payne
J P	Isobel Pero
I · P (×2)	John Pero
I · P / J P	John Pollock
I · Q / I · 2 / J 2	John Quantock
I R (×5)	John Reily
I R	Isaac Ribouleau
J R (×3)	John Rich
I R / I · R / I · R	John Robins
J R	John Roker
I S / J · S	John H. Le Sage

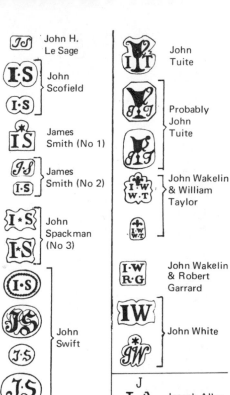

John H. Le Sage

John Scofield

James Smith (No 1)

James Smith (No 2)

John Spackman (No 3)

John Swift

James Tookey

John Tuite

John Tuite

Probably John Tuite

John Wakelin & William Taylor

John Wakelin & Robert Garrard

John White

Joseph Allen

Joseph (No 1) & John Angell

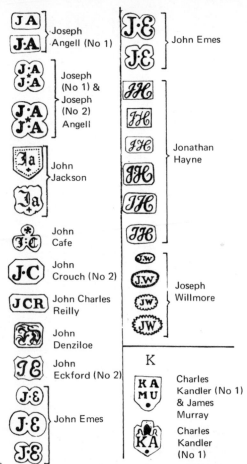

Mark	Maker
J A	Joseph Angell (No 1)
J·A	
J:A / J:A	Joseph (No 1) & Joseph (No 2) Angell
J*A / J*A	
Ja	John Jackson
Ja	
I·C	John Cafe
J·C	John Crouch (No 2)
JCR	John Charles Reilly
JD	John Denziloe
JE	John Eckford (No 2)
J·E	John Emes
J·E	
J·E	
J·E	John Emes
J·E	
J·H	Jonathan Hayne
J·W	Joseph Willmore

K

Mark	Maker
KA MU	Charles Kandler (No 1) & James Murray
KA	Charles Kandler (No 1)

Charles F. Kandler

L

 John Ladyman

 George Lambe

 Jane Lambe

 Jonathan Lambe

 Paul De Lamerie

 Probably Paul De Lamerie

 Louisa P. Courtauld

 Louisa P. Courtauld & George Cowles

 Louisa P. Courtauld &

 Samuel Courtauld (No 2)

 Samuel Lea

 Ralph Leake

 Samuel Lee

 John Leech

 ⎤
 ⎥ Lewis Hamon
 ⎦

 Isaac Liger

⎤
⎥ Louis Laroche
⎦

397

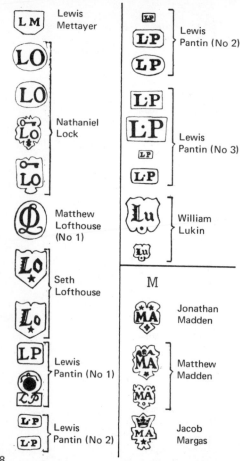

Lewis Mettayer

Nathaniel Lock

Matthew Lofthouse (No 1)

Seth Lofthouse

Lewis Pantin (No 1)

Lewis Pantin (No 2)

Lewis Pantin (No 2)

Lewis Pantin (No 3)

William Lukin

M

Jonathan Madden

Matthew Madden

Jacob Margas

Samuel Margas

 John Matthew

 Mary Matthew

 William Matthew (No 1)

 William Matthew (No 2)

 Mary Chawner

 Mary Chawner & George W. Adams

 Matthew Cooper

 Lewis Mettayer

 Magdalen Feline

 Mordecai Fox

 Mary Hyde & John Reily

 Mary Lofthouse

Matthew Lofthouse (No 1)

399

Andrew Moore

 Thomas Morse

 Mary Pantin

 Mary Piers

 Matthew Roker

 Mary Sumner

 Mary & Elizabeth Sumner

 Mary & Elizabeth Sumner

N

 Nicholas Clausen

 Antony Nelme

 Antony Nelme

 Francis Nelme

 Nicholas Sprimont

 Nicholas Sprimont

O

 Charles Overing

James Overing

P

 Peter Archambo (No 1)

Peter Archambo (No 2) & Peter Meure

400

Mark
Paillet

 Simon
Pantin
(No 1)

 Thomas
Parr
(No 1)

 Humphrey
Payne

 Peter &
Jonathan
Bateman

 Peter &
Ann
Bateman

 Peter, Ann
& William
Bateman

 Peter &
William
Bateman

 Pierre
Bouteiller

 Pierre
Le Cheaube

 Peter
Courtauld

 Paul Crespin

Paul Crespin

 Edmund Pearce

 John Pero

 Jean Petry

Philip Garden

 Pierre Gillois

 Paul Hanet

 Pezé Pilleau

 Peter Jouet

 Paul De Lamerie

 Paul De Lamerie

 Pierre Platel

 Pezé Pilleau

 Philip Platel

402

Philip
Rainaud

 Philip
Rundell

 Philip
Roker
(No 2)

Paul
Storr

 Phillip
Roker (No 3)

 Philip
Rollos (No 2)

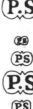

Philip
Rundell

403

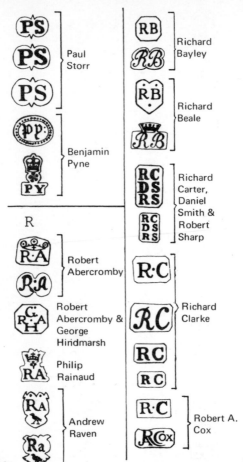

Paul Storr

Benjamin Pyne

R

Robert Abercromby

Robert Abercromby & George Hindmarsh

Philip Rainaud

Andrew Raven

Richard Bayley

Richard Beale

Richard Carter, Daniel Smith & Robert Sharp

Richard Clarke

Robert A. Cox

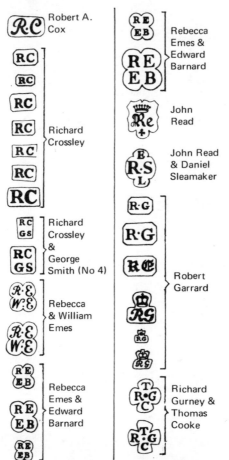

Robert A. Cox

Richard Crossley

Richard Crossley & George Smith (No 4)

Rebecca & William Emes

Rebecca Emes & Edward Barnard

Rebecca Emes & Edward Barnard

John Read

John Read & Daniel Sleamaker

Robert Garrard

Richard Gurney & Thomas Cooke

405

Richard Gurney & Thomas Cooke

    Robert Hennell (No 1)

 Robert Hennell (No 1) & David Hennell (No 2)

Robert Hennell (No 1) David Hennell (No 2) & Samuel Hennell

 Robert Hennell (No 1) & Samuel Hennell

 Robert Hennell (No 2)

 John Scofield & Robert Jones

 Isaac Ribouleau

 Richard Kersill

 Robert Makepeace (No 1) & Richard Carter

 Robert Makepeace (No 2)

 Robert (No 2) & Thomas Makepeace

 Philip Roker (No 1)

Philip Roker (No 2)

 406

Philip
Rollos (No 1)

 Philip
Rollos (No 2)

R·R Richard
Rugg (No 1)

R·R Richard
Rugg (No 2)

 Richard
Scarlett

 Robert
Sharp

 Richard
Sibley (No 1)

RW Richard
Watts

 Richard
Watts

S

S·A
SA
SA
SA
SA
SA
S·A
S·A
S·A
SA
SA
SA
S·A

Stephen
Adams
(No 1)

407

Stephen Adams (No 1)

 Stephen Adams (No 2)

 John H. Le Sage

 Samuel Courtauld (No 1)

 Sebastian & James Crespel

 Richard Scarlett

William Scarlett

 Samuel Godbehere

 Samuel Godbehere & Edward Wigan

 Samuel Godbehere, Edward Wigan, & James Bult

 Samuel Godbehere & James Bult

Samuel Hennell

Samuel Hennell

  Samuel Hennell & John Terry

 Sarah Holaday

  Samuel Hutton

 Sarah Hutton

 William Shaw (No 1)

 Alice Sheene

 Joseph Sheene

 Probably Simon Jouet

   Simon Jouet

 Samuel Lea

 Samuel Lee

  Simon Le Sage

Daniel Sleamaker

Gabriel Sleath

Samuel Margas

James Smith (No 1)

Simon Pantin (No 1)

Simon Pantin (No 2)

Sarah Parr

John Spackman (No 1)

Thomas Spackman (No 1)

Thomas Spackman (No 1)

William Spackman (No 1)

Francis Spilsbury

Samuel Smith

Samuel Taylor

John Sutton

Thomas Sutton

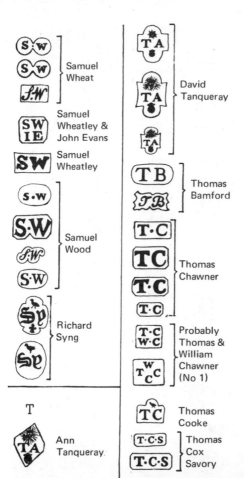

Samuel Wheat

Samuel Wheatley & John Evans

Samuel Wheatley

Samuel Wood

Richard Syng

Ann Tanqueray

David Tanqueray

Thomas Bamford

Thomas Chawner

Probably Thomas & William Chawner (No 1)

Thomas Cooke

Thomas Cox Savory

Mark	Maker
T.C.S	Thomas Cox Savory
TE R·S	Thomas Ellerton & Richard Sibley (No 1)
TE R·S	
TF	Thomas Farren
T F	Thomas Folkingham
T·G	Thomas Gilpin
T.G	
TG IG IC	Thomas Guest, Joseph Guest & Joseph Craddock
TG IG IC	
	Probably
T·H I·C	Thomas Hannam & John Crouch (No 1)
TH IC	
TH	Thomas Hayter
TH	

Mark	Maker
T·H	Thomas Hayter
T·H	
TH GH	Thomas & George Hayter
TH GH	
TH GH	
T·H	Thomas Heming
T·H	Probably Thomas Hemming
TM	Thomas Morse
T*N	Thomas Northcote
T·N	
T·N	
T·N	
TN	
TN	
TN	
TN	
TN	

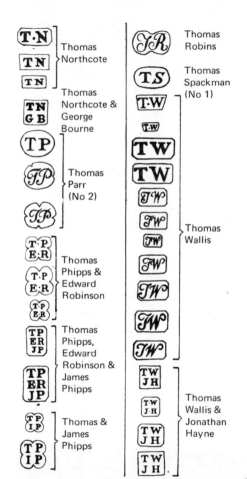

Thomas Northcote

Thomas Northcote & George Bourne

Thomas Parr (No 2)

Thomas Phipps & Edward Robinson

Thomas Phipps, Edward Robinson & James Phipps

Thomas & James Phipps

Thomas Robins

Thomas Spackman (No 1)

Thomas Wallis

Thomas Wallis & Jonathan Hayne

413

Thomas Whipham

 Thomas Whipham & William Williams

 Thomas Whipham & Charles Wright

Probably Thomas Whipham & Charles Wright

 Thomas Wright (No 1)

 Thomas Wright (No 2)

W

 William Abdy (Nos 1 & 2)

W A

WA

 WA

 WA

 WA

 WA

 W·A

w·A

WA William Abdy (Nos 1 & 2)

 Joseph Ward

 Richard Watts

 William Bateman (No 1)

William Bateman (No 1)

 William Bateman (No 2)

William Bateman (No 2) & Daniel Ball

William Bell

 William Bell

William Bellassyse

 Walter Brind

 William Burwash

 William Burwash & Richard Sibley (No 1)

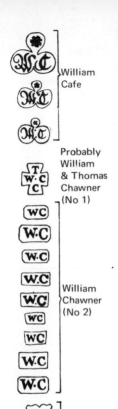

William Cafe

Probably William & Thomas Chawner (No 1)

William Chawner (No 2)

William Cripps

William Eaton (Nos 1 & 2)

William Eley (No 1) & George Pierrepont

William Eley (No 1)

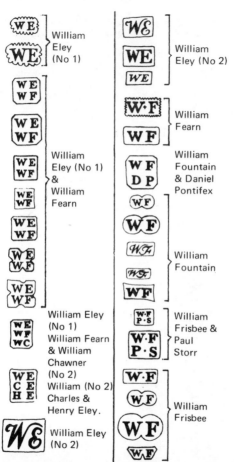

William Eley (No 1)

William Eley (No 2)

William Eley (No 1) & William Fearn

William Fearn

William Fountain & Daniel Pontifex

William Fountain

William Eley (No 1) William Fearn & William Chawner (No 2) William (No 2) Charles & Henry Eley.

William Frisbee & Paul Storr

William Eley (No 2)

William Frisbee

William
Frisbee

 William
& John
Frisbee

 William
Gould

 William
Grundy

 William
Grundy &
Edward
Fernell

John
White

 William
Jury &
Stephen
Adams
(No 1)

 George
Wickes

 David
Willaume
(No 1)

 David
Willaume
(No 2)

 William
Kersill

418

William Lukin

 William Matthew (No 2)

 Edward Wood

 William Peaston

 William & Robert Peaston

 William Plummer

 Possibly William & James Priest

 William K. Reid

 William K. Reid

 William Sampel

 William Scarlett

 William Shaw (No 1)

 William Shaw (No 2)

William Shaw (No 2) & William Priest

419

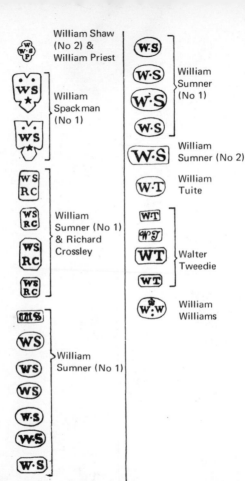

William Shaw (No 2) & William Priest

William Spackman (No 1)

William Sumner (No 1) & Richard Crossley

William Sumner (No 1)

William Sumner (No 1)

William Sumner (No 2)

William Tuite

Walter Tweedie

William Williams

420